Dean M. Frieders

Foundations of
Sustainable Development

Law, Regulation, and Planning

D1496119

SECTION OF **REAL** | **TRUST &**
PROPERTY | **ESTATE LAW**

Defending Liberty
Pursuing Justice

Cover design by Sonya Taylor/ABA Publishing.

Printed in the United States of America.

16 15 14 13 12   5 4 3 2 1

Library of Congress Cataloging-in-Publication Data

Foundations of Sustainable Development /
edited by Dean Frieders.
    p. cm.
  Includes bibliographical references and index.
  ISBN 978-1-61438-325-3 (print : alk. paper) — ISBN 978-1-61438-326-0
(ebook)
  1. Sustainable development—Law and legislation—United States. 2.
City planning and redevelopment law—United States. 3. Public works—Law
and legislation—United States. 4. Environmental engineering—United
States. 5. Building laws—United States. 6. Sustainable design—United
States. I. Frieders, Dean.
  KF5505.L39 2012
  343.7307'4—dc23

                                                            2011052205

Contents

About the Author

Dean M. Frieders is a licensed attorney in Illinois, and a partner at the Aurora, Illinois, lawfirm of Mickey, Wilson, Weiler, Renzi & Andersson, P.C. He is a graduate of North Central College, *summa cum laude*, and Chicago-Kent College of Law, *with honors*. He has been selected as a Rising Star lawyer in the field of local government law by the Superlawyers organization in 2009, 2010, and 2011.

Dean is a frequent lecturer and the author of numerous articles that have been published by a number of bar associations, the Illinois Municipal League, the Illinois Institute for Local Government Law, and the National School Board Association Council of School Attorneys. He was the founder and served as Chairman of the Northern Illinois University Sustainable Governance Conference. In addition, Dean has worked as a licensed Firefighter/EMT, and brings his practical experience as a first responder to benefit his clients.

He is a certified arbitrator and guardian ad litem, and has advanced a number of municipal law cases through the circuit and appellate courts in Illinois, establishing important new laws regarding land development, zoning, and annexation agreements. He has also served as both counsel to and an appointed member of numerous county and municipal electoral boards, and has served as a Special Assistant State's Attorney to represent public officials in municipal litigation.

He has been responsible for annexation agreements resulting in the annexation and development of tens of thousands of acres, and has worked to include sustainable governance practices in those annexation agreements, including the development of new and innovative stormwater management techniques, creative incentives for eco-friendly development, and alternative methods of contracting for environmental-related services such as LEED building engineering and design. Dean lives in Northern Illinois with his lovely wife Dana, his beautiful daughter, Lulu, and the world's most intelligent Miniature Schnauzer, Dharma. In his free time, he hikes, skis, explores the Midwest via bicycle, and spends time with his family. Dean may be reached at: *dean@frieders.com.*

Acknowledgments

This book would not have been possible without the patient guidance of its primary editor, Cynthia Boyer Blakeslee, who channeled the enthusiasm of a novice author into the complete book that you see today. With a rare combination of technical mastery of the written word and a keen sense of flow and literary rhythm, her help was invaluable. In addition, Jeffrey Salyards and his staff at the American Bar Association worked in earnest to translate a manuscript into an actual book. I am indebted to each of them, and thank them for making this project better than I could have created alone.

In addition, I have to thank my parents, Ronald and Denise Frieders, lifelong farmers in Northern Illinois. When your life and living come from farming the same piece of land year in and year out, you have a powerful incentive to ensure that your methods and practices are sustainable. My parents showed me what it meant to be active environmentalists, instead of environmental activists; they imbued me with a deep reverence for the earth and its many blessings. They also gave me the best gifts that one could hope for: my brilliant sister, Daun Biewenga (and her husband Mike, whom I've spent many an afternoon chasing on bikes and skis), and my brother, Ryan Frieders. Ryan is my best friend and role model. He inspires me each day with his selflessness and generosity, and by carrying on our multi-generational family tradition of farming. This book is written with the hopes that smarter development can limit sprawl, and can preserve quiet country roads, tall, green cornfields, and peaceful farmsteads where his crops and family will grow.

At the risk of cliché, I cannot overstate the significance that the support of my wife, Dana Frieders, has had—upon this book, my professional career, and my life in general. She has stood behind me when I needed support, beside me when I needed a friend, and in front of me when I needed a guardian. She is the reason for my every success, the solace for my every challenge, and the reward for my every accomplishment. I have been lucky beyond words to have found a dingledodie that I can humbly shamble after. Dana not only puts up with my busy work schedule and the demands of researching and writing a book—she also raises our wonderful daughter, Lucille Louise.

Lulu is the genesis of this book, as she is the genesis of all things in my life since her birth. While all parents believe their children to be beautiful, gifted, clever, and poetic, I have the great fortune of knowing it to be true of my daughter. The greatest joys of my life have been seeing her smile, hearing her laugh, and learning from her as she absorbs all of the knowledge in the world. Since her birth, I try harder to be the man that she believes me to be. She makes me not only want to be better myself, but also to create a better world to share with her. I can't help but think that any parent who looks into their child's eyes *must want to create a better* future. She has taught me to question all things, and to look at the world with a childish sense of wonder— to embrace change, to see and protect nature all around me, and to be more original, more creative, and more responsible.

In the end, this book, as with everything I do, is for Dana and Lulu, the two great loves of my life.

1

Understanding Sustainability: Steps Toward a Successful Project

This book is intended to be a guide to understanding sustainable projects. While crafted from the viewpoint of a practitioner involved predominantly in public development and the laws applicable to units of government, the discussion applies with equal force to both public and private entities, and to large groups and individual stakeholders.

The subsequent chapters of this book explore specific sustainable development techniques. This exploration is not done with a goal of expansively describing the engineering or legal aspects of such techniques, but rather in an attempt to identify and explain some of the many tools available for inclusion in the toolkit of someone hoping to employ sustainable development within their community or project. The book provides a description of the techniques utilized, phrased in such a fashion as to be understood without having an engineering degree. It also identifies some of the common pitfalls and explores methods of addressing those issues using the most readily available methods that either a developer, a public body, or a regulatory agency has available: laws and regulations, contracts, and design requirements.

To be able to build a collection of ideas that can be implemented within specific projects, the planners, lawyers, or public officials undertaking a sustainable project must understand what sustainability is, they must be able to identify the actual goals for the project, and they must be able to put together a team of individuals who understand both the project and the goals.

WHAT IS SUSTAINABILITY?

For at least the past 40 years, the United States has been increasingly direct about recognizing and discussing environmentalism as a social issue. It might come as a surprise to some, but it was not until 1969 that the US Environmental Protection Agency was created. The first Clean Water Act followed shortly thereafter in 1972 and, for the first time, nationwide legislation sought to improve the quality and safety of water, and the federal government began imposing additional environmental regulations in earnest.

Over time, the concept of environmental regulation became one that spawned many controversies—including numerous disputes over animal habitat, logging practices, use and disposal of hazardous material, and other areas where property rights and commercial interests seemed to be at odds with environmental policies. But with the passage of time, many units of local government, including schools, municipalities, counties, and others, have begun to embrace environmentalism at a micro level. Though there is no federal law requiring local buildings to be LEED (Leadership in Energy and Environmental Design) certified, public buildings are being designed and constructed to those standards at an increasing rate.

The changes in perception and the importance of environmental issues are not limited to governments; the social importance of these issues is growing at a rapid rate. Companies work to develop and market "green" products made from renewable resources and products that lessen energy consumption, and then market these products to show how environmentally friendly they are. In its many forms, environmentalism and the concept of sustainability is increasingly important for commercial, social, and governmental interests.

What exactly is sustainability? Webster's defines sustainable as "1: capable of being sustained; 2a: of, relating to, or being a method of harvesting or using a resource so that the resource is not permanently depleted or permanently damaged <sustainable techniques> <sustainable agriculture>, b: of or relating to a lifestyle involving the use of sustainable methods <sustainable society>."[1] If sustainability was strictly defined in the absolute terms of the dictionary, much of what society has come to view as sustainable would not be. For example, hybrid cars that use gasoline engines supplemented by batteries and electric motors might be popularly viewed as sustainable, but they still use gasoline. They do not use fossil fuels in such a way that the resource is not permanently depleted; they simply deplete the resource at a slower rate.

Sustainability, then, has to be taken with a flexible definition. In popular culture, sustainability includes not only those techniques that prevent permanent depletion of resources, but also methods that reduce the rate of consumption of resources. Constructing a super-insulated building will not, by itself, eliminate the use of external energy to heat and/or cool the building, but it will (should) result in reduced energy use. Building a windmill will not eliminate fossil fuel consumption in a given area, but it should reduce the amount of fossil fuels otherwise needed to generate the energy produced and converted by the windmill. Both of these projects, by nearly any contemporary definition of the word, would be viewed as being sustainable.

---

1. Merriam Webster Online Dictionary, Sustainable. Accessed Apr. 16, 2010. http://www.merriam-webster.com/dictionary/sustainable.

Over the past few decades, sustainability has been invoked in defense of many things. Many believe that the continuing reliance of modern society on fossil fuels and industrial production contributes to global warming, acid rain, and the melting of the polar ice caps (among other environmental items in the contemporary parade of horribles). In response, sustainable techniques have been introduced and popularized as a means of hopefully slowing, halting, or even reversing some of the environmental damage that science tells us has occurred over the past century. In areas prone to flooding, sustainable engineering has been popularized as a means of providing storm water and flood water control that minimizes damage to natural or man-made environments. These sort of projects, aimed directly at mitigating or eliminating society's impact on nature, or at mitigating nature's impact on society, are the projects that are most often branded with the sustainability label. This form of sustainability can perhaps best be viewed as a response, whether proactive or reactive, to an environmental crisis.

When communities look to construct a LEED-certified building, or when industries spend research and development monies on developing sustainable technologies, quite frequently the underlying goal is not environmentalism, but rather capitalism. A municipality might be legitimately concerned about reducing energy consumption and might appreciate the public relations benefits of being able to discuss the environmental benefits of sustainable buildings. However, the practical discussion as to whether a given project should be designed and built with traditional construction or with sustainable construction often focuses on the reduced operating costs of the sustainable project in the long term. A community might like the fact that a naturalized area planted with prairie grass and flowers provides comparatively cheap opportunities for storm water infiltration, but they *love* not having to budget to mow such areas on a weekly basis. With increasing energy costs, sustainability can be viewed in many instances as a response to an economic crisis. Sustainability is coming at communities from all sides—from public concerns about water quality and land development, to public regulations restricting the disposal of computers, printers, and other technology.[2]

Another form of sustainability that has been advanced a great deal has been the concept of sustainability as a "simpler way of living." The ability to live "off the grid" in a self-reliant fashion has been advanced as a response to the hustle and complexity of modern life. This form of sustainability is, quite simply, a reactionary social movement aimed at reducing the need to rely on outside resources and assistance.

Perhaps the most interesting form of sustainable development is that which is sustainable to be sustainable—or which is branded as sustainable to reap the benefits of being perceived as such. Companies and governments alike have shown an increasing willingness to undertake projects that they *describe* as being sustainable or environmentally friendly, for the purpose of obtaining the positive response, social benefits, and increased marketability associated with a "sustainable" project. The good news is that whatever the motivation for a sustainable project might be, if it truly is sustainable, then environmental benefits—in addition to the commercial benefits—should result. The bad news is that altogether too often, it appears as if companies engage in *greenwashing*, which is the taking of a nonsustainable product or project and marketing it as being sustainable for the purpose of obtaining some positive benefit.[3]

---

2. See, e.g., Illinois Public Act 095-0959, Electronic Products Recycling and Reuse Act, regulating the disposal of electronic devices such as computers, televisions, printers, and related items.

3. Greenwashing claims are actually one of the newer forms of litigation to arise out of the sustainability/environmentalism movement. Greenwashing claims effectively seek to prove, for example, that the manufacturer of a given product is misleading the public about how environmentally friendly that product actually is. For example, in *Paduano v. American Honda Motor Co., Inc.*, 88 Cal. Rptr.3d 90 (Cal. Ct. App. 2009), the owner of a hybrid car sued the

It is the desire to appear to be "green" or "eco-friendly" that has given rise to cars that are ostensibly "hybrid" cars, but that are hybrid only in the most technical of senses. For example, at the date of publication, Lexus offered the LS600h hybrid, starting at a base price of $108,000. This vehicle is equipped with a 5.0L v-8 and a hybrid supplement; it is capable of going from 0 to 60 mph in 5.5 seconds. However, its EPA rated combined city/highway mileage is only 21 mpg—a figure that can be exceeded by some small sport utility vehicles and many cars, and that is scarcely better than the 19 mpg garnered by the nonhybrid version of that same car.[4] There are those who argue that expensive implementations of hybrid automobile technology are the only ways to cover the costs of engineering and refining the technology to a point that it can be included in less expensive automobiles. Regardless of the truth or falsity of that defense, one of the premises of this book is that those who are truly interested in sustainable development are interested for the purpose of actually *being sustainable*, rather than just being able to put a green badge on an otherwise not sustainable project.

▓▓ IDENTIFYING YOUR GOALS ▓▓

Where the purpose of providing a "sustainable" product is solely, or even predominantly, to increase its marketability and sale rates (resulting in increased consumption of resources to manufacture and distrib-

---

manufacturer when the car failed to produce the mileage ratings the manufacturer had specified. In *Koh v. SC Johnson & Son, Inc.*, Case No. 5:2009cv00927 (N.D. Cal. 2009), a consumer filed suit against SC Johnson, claiming that their "greenlist" labeling of products was misleading. Tim Clayton, *Preventing Greenwashing Lawsuits*, OHIO GREEN BUILDING LAW (Jan. 17, 2010), http:// ohiogreenbuildinglaw.com/2010/01/17/preventing-greenwashing-lawsuits/.

4. Lexus website, LS Hybrid 2012. http://www.lexus.com/models/LSh/detailed_ specifications.html, accessed March 21, 2010.

ute the product), it is difficult to see how such efforts can reasonably be labeled as being sustainable. Certainly, if the product is replacing or supplementing another consumable that is significantly less environmentally sound, there might be an argument to be made. But one of the central theses to be advanced in this book is the notion that being "green" for the purpose of marketing one's environmental sensitivity is often a misguided goal. Instead, those who wish to undertake a sustainable project should do so using a pragmatic approach. They should evaluate the *actual cost and benefit* of sustainable aspects of the project. Where the goal of a project is to get a certain green label, the outcome might not be as environmentally friendly as if the goal of the project is to complete it in a sustainable fashion.

Aside from products that are greenwashed without actually being sustainable, what all of these different takes on sustainability *should* have in common is that they all *should* provide positive environmental benefits, and they all *should* reduce the use of nonrenewable resources. There is an inherent conflict, however, in the method by which sustainable projects are evaluated after completion. LEED building standards are an easy target to explore this conflict because they have defined standards and because they are reasonably well known and accepted as being "sustainable."

Assume for a moment that a town is undertaking construction of a new public building in a relatively rural area. At the outset of the project, an enthusiastic architect convinces the town government that LEED construction is environmentally, economically, and socially responsible, and the long-term benefits of the construction outweigh any additional short-term increases in design or construction costs. While the LEED system will be explored in greater detail in subsequent chapters, a great (and perhaps even unfair) simplification of the process is that a building is given points for having various sustainable techniques incorporated into its design. Depending upon the total number of points accumulated in the design and construction of the building, it might not be eligible for certification at all, or it might be eligible for one of the various different levels of LEED certification. Among the construction techniques rewarded with points under the LEED program is the recycling of construction debris.

At the time of constructing the project, the town has two choices. One choice is to haul the debris to a landfill that is ten miles away. The other choice is to haul the debris to a recycling center in the nearest large urban center, which is 200 miles away. Under this circumstance, if the goal is LEED accreditation, the only answer might be to haul the debris 20 times as far and to expend 20 times as much fossil fuel, create 20 times as much exhaust from the trucks being utilized, and so forth. That may or may not be the outcome that is actually more environmentally sensitive and more sustainable. But what if the goal is more simply defined? What if the goal is to construct a sustainable building? If the town is not constrained by meeting a certain defined standard, it might evaluate this decision differently and might determine that under these circumstances it makes more sense to dispose of the materials instead of recycling them. The town might determine that it makes more sense to spend the money on tangible improvements to the building rather than on hauling recyclable materials several hundred miles. Those improvements might actually reduce energy consumption and maintenance need over the building's lifetime.

The point of this thought exercise is not to set up a LEED straw man and then knock it down; the LEED program is a great one and is one that sets up a tangible system that rewards environmental stewardship and encourages building owners to incorporate sustainable design into their projects. Rather, the point of this exercise is to suggest that when a "sustainable" project is undertaken, the parties responsible for its planning and implementation should define their goals clearly. If the goal is to obtain LEED certification, for any of the numerous reasons one might want to obtain such certification, then their conduct, their contracts, and their focus should be on obtaining that goal. If, on the other hand, the goal is to complete a sustainable project, while LEED certification might be one way of measuring success, they should evaluate and make decisions throughout the building process keeping in mind *the goal of being sustainable* rather than working toward accumulating points or obtaining positive public relations.

Moreover, if the goal is to be sustainable, then when the parties planning the project get to the point of making a project decision, they should evaluate that decision from the proper perspective and based on the unique characteristics of the project. Does spending money on permeable pavement make good sense to address a given project's storm water needs? Permeable pavement might require extra maintenance, special snow removal equipment, or other future expenditures. Depending on the nature of the local soils and the material used, the pores in the material that make it permeable might become plugged and render it less effective or ineffective as a permeable area. On a small site, permeable pavement might nonetheless make sense, both from an economic and environmental perspective. But if there is a large site and a community or developer can construct other forms of sustainable storm water management (such as bioswales, aquifer recharge, and infiltration basins), then there might be more effective and less expensive means of meeting the goal of being sustainable. There is no "one size fits all" solution to all sustainability issues.

It is likely a reality that any justification for undertaking a sustainable project is better than not undertaking a sustainable project at all. If the outcome is good, the ends might justify the means. But this is a time of rising energy costs and of an increasing consensus regarding the impact that communities have on the environment (and the likely long-term social costs associated with that impact). Anyone who wishes to undertake a project of this nature—whether it be called sustainable, green, environmentally friendly, or otherwise—should not have to look very far to find both a justification for the green bent to the project or to identify worthwhile goals to be achieved through the completion of the project.

If a group wishes to have a successful project, the compass that guides its project from start to finish must be a clearly defined and expressly identified goal. If the goal is to complete the project in a sustainable fashion, then let sustainability be the guide.

▦ ASSEMBLING A TEAM ▦

Extending the metaphor from the last paragraph even further, if the goal serves as the compass that guides the project, then the project team is the group that crews the ship and enables the project to set sail toward completion. When undertaking a sustainable project, in all likelihood the project owner will need to retain some consultants who have specific experience with projects of that nature—and will need to integrate them with the balance of a team who might not have specific experience in developing sustainable projects.

Talking with other professionals involved in a sustainable development project at the outset and at regular intervals during the course of the project is invaluable in enabling each member of the team to understand his or her role. Accordingly, once the project owner understands its own goals, assembling a team approach to sustainable projects is one of the best ways to implement techniques necessary to achieve those goals.

For example, continue to assume that a town is working on the sustainable building project discussed above. One component of the construction process will be the design of sustainable systems by engineers and architects. One component will be the drafting of contracts that provide the requirements for the performance of all obligations relating to the construction (and the prerequisites to payment for those services). One component will be the selection and hiring of contractors to perform those services. One component will be the selection and purchase of materials necessary for the construction. Finally, one component will be having staff and officials review and approve the foregoing. Ideally, all of these components mesh together neatly and produce a sustainable project that comes in on time and on budget. For that to happen, everyone involved in the project needs to understand (1) the master goals of the project; (2) the nature of the project; (3) their role in the project; and, (4) the impact the goals for and nature of the project will have upon their work.

The attorney working on the project customarily prepares contracts and other similar agreements for use in the construction process. If those contracts are to be for a standard building, traditional Architects Institute of America (AIA) contracts might be used, albeit with modifications. But if the attorney understands the goal to be building either a sustainable building, or a sustainable building that obtains LEED certification, that dramatically changes the approach to be taken and the documents to be used. Even if AIA contracts are used, they must be modified in fundamental ways. A single, seemingly minor error by a contractor during the course of the project can result in the failure of the entire building to obtain LEED certification. And that can cause hundreds of thousands or even millions of dollars of losses over the lifetime of the project.

But simply telling the attorney that the goal is a LEED-certified building is not enough. The attorney, engineer, architect, LEED commissioning agent, construction manager, and others involved in the project need to meet before bids are let so that they ensure the bid specifications adequately identify and mandate compliance with the LEED regulations. The public works department or maintenance crew needs to be involved so that they can indicate what sort of maintenance training they will need and so that they can understand what warranties are being provided. Each member of the team needs to understand the role of the others. Will the construction manager be responsible for ensuring contractors use the right materials and the appropriate, environmentally sensitive construction techniques, or does that fall to the commissioning agent? What happens if a given sustainable design element is not practical to actually construct? When does risk of loss transfer to the owner for expensive items like the chillers and HVAC equipment? What happens if the building is constructed and does not ultimately perform to design specifications?

The list of potential questions and issues is lengthy. Ultimately, no building owner will be able to predict and prevent every issue that could ever arise during the construction and occupancy of the building. But in the course of working on projects such as this, a surprising thing happens when the building owner convenes a pre-bid, preconstruction meeting of the consultants and staffers involved in the project and provides an express, stated set of goals for the project: everyone works to achieve those goals. The approach that each party takes to a project is different if the project is to "construct a new building," compared to if the project is to "construct a sustainable building that endeavors to be LEED certified, but that favors sustainability over strict point accumulation."

Convening the team is essential to the process. As the team grows with the addition of contractors and subcontractors, additional team meetings must be called. In the vast majority of completed construction projects, the only time that the attorneys responsible for the project meet contractors and subcontractors (other than the general contractor and a few prime contract holders) is when there is litigation following the project. If a project owner wants to get its contractors' and subcontractors' attention, it should have a preconstruction "team" meeting with them where the project attorney explains the liquidated damages and other consequences that would be imposed for even a minor deviation from the sustainability specifications for the project.

It is impossible to control every action taken by every person involved in the workings of a construction site. But if a project owner approaches the whole process with the idea of informing the team of a set of stated objectives, it should be able to avoid a situation where someone later claims not to have known that what he did was not permitted.

Throughout the course of this book, there will be examples of the best-case and worst-case scenarios. These examples are developed both out of imagining the best and worst that can happen, and also out of real events and cases. Does it seem implausible that one would have to choose between disposing of building materials within ten miles or recycling building materials 200 miles away? That example is taken from an actual LEED-certified building project in the midwestern United States. Does it seem unlikely that a single, apparent mistake by a building contractor could both be irreparable *and* generate hundreds of thousands of dollars of losses? Ask the contractor who tried to collect $50,000 in unpaid construction costs and who was hit with a countersuit for $1.3 million in damages (a majority of which related to the failure to achieve LEED accreditation, allegedly caused by a minor contractor mistake).

Public entities and those who work with public entities are accustomed to addressing adversity and controlling behavior with regulations and restrictions, and permits and processes. They instinctively understand that there are some groups subject to their control and some entities that have a superior governmental mandate and can potentially regulate them. But there are some areas where all persons, regardless of their association or lawful entitlements, are placed on common ground—subject to the same requirements. The laws of nature apply to us all.

2

Laying the Foundation for Sustainable Development with Codes and Ordinances

People tend to regard sustainability and related concepts as new inventions and as man's ingenious response to modern economic and environmental pressures. In fact, many sustainable design concepts date back to the earliest civilizations. The Code of Hammurabi not only regulated social conduct, but it also prescribed penalties for building an unsafe or unpermitted structure.[1] These rules were designed to preserve lives and to create accountability in an industry that had previously been unregulated. To promote safety and commerce, Greek and Roman laws as early as 4 BC regulated land use and required the creation of *agoras*, or public squares, along with restricting uses of properties surrounding such squares.[2]

Perhaps the earliest attempt at a consistent *set* of land use regulations is found in the Laws of the Indies, established by King Phillip II of Spain in 1573. These laws were intended to regulate the

---

1. Emily Talen, *Design by the Rules*, 75 J. AM. PLANNING ASS'N 144, 147 (2009).
2. *Id.*

development of Spanish colonies in the Americas. They included rules for site selection, development of communities around a central plaza, restrictions on building and roadway sizes and setbacks, and other similar provisions aimed at maximizing commercial opportunities and ensuring that colonized cities had long-term usefulness.[3] In the seventeenth century, Daniel Stoelpart developed a master Regulating Plan for the City of Amsterdam, which dictated the location of public buildings, canals, streets, and residences, and which was accompanied by a companion ordinance establishing basic regulations for building design and construction, along with sanitation and public health.[4]

Many cities developed at and after these times were constructed pursuant to a master plan that was intended to regulate construction and provide for public safety and welfare. At the same time, however, early governments struggled with the conflict between public regulation and private land use rights. In the United States, private land use rights often superseded the public interest. In retrospect, it was the relative absence of regulations that permitted property owners to construct wholly untenable developments and projects—projects that ultimately forced the hand of municipalities and forced the creation of more stringent zoning and development codes.

In 1915, the 42-story Equitable Building was constructed in Lower Manhattan, making use of steel beam construction and elevators. The shadow from the building covered seven acres of ground, thus greatly diminishing the value of surrounding properties. The building had zero setbacks; the property was built to 42 stories of height across the entire property.[5]

---

3. *Id. See also* http://parentseyes.arizona.edu/adobe/townmaking.html (last visited October 16, 2011).
4. Talen, *supra* note 1, at 148.
5. NEW YORK CITY, DEP'T OF CITY PLANNING, History. www.nyc.gov/html/dcp/html/zone/zonehis.shtml (last visited Feb. 10, 2010).

At the same time, high demand for immigrant housing generated the construction of high-density tenement housing. Demand for industrial production generated warehouses and factories encroaching on all areas of New York City, including approaching Fifth Avenue. As a result, New York City passed the Zoning Resolution of 1916, its first zoning control. The Zoning Resolution imposed restrictions on all forms of building, from tenement buildings to skyscrapers. However, the densities contemplated by this original zoning ordinance were quite unrealistic; according to New York City Government, buildout under that code would have permitted 55,000,000 to live within New York City—but automobile travel would have been greatly impeded. After much debate, New York City eventually replaced the entire Zoning Code in 1961. Modern New York City Zoning includes three basic districts (residential, commercial and manufacturing), which are each divided into varying densities and permitted/special/prohibited uses.[6]

The story of the development of the first New York City zoning codes parallels the experience of many communities. Zoning and building regulations were reactive—these early twentieth-century ordinances sprung out of a desire to prohibit the recurrence of some project or event that had already occurred. Municipalities had forgotten the example of the Laws of the Indies and other similar zoning code precursors that affirmatively established rules to proactively create a desired outcome.

When trying to govern any subject with regulations, there are two potential ways to accomplish the desired result. One way is to indicate what outcome or conduct is permissible. The other way is to prohibit conduct that is impermissible. Assume that a town wants to impose regulations to require the production of brown cardboard boxes that are one foot by one foot by one foot in dimension and are capable of safely holding a 20-pound package. It would seem sensible to write a regulation that says just that: specify the required or permitted

---

6. *Id.*

dimensions, indicate the required color scheme, and specify a minimum strength or capacity. Or maybe the town could provide a color, scale drawing of the box, with measurements and characteristics.

The other way to write the regulation would be to prohibit all other types of boxes. This regulation would prohibit boxes that are blue, red, green, yellow, purple, orange, and so on. It would prohibit boxes that are capable of holding only one to 19 pounds, along with boxes capable of holding 21 or more pounds. It would prohibit boxes that are oval, cylindrical, pyramid-shaped, spherical, oblong, and so forth. It would prohibit boxes with specified dimensions that are too small and boxes with specified dimensions that are too large. The regulations would also prohibit the use of leather, wood (other than wood pulp), bone, plastic, steel, aluminum, titanium, composite materials, and more as the materials used in production of the box. Eventually, one could put together a set of regulations that produce the desired outcome by exhaustively prohibiting all other forms of boxes. Once the regulation was passed, however, the town would find that it had not prohibited every other possible color, and someone would, much to its chagrin, start producing boxes that were chartreuse . . . or that were capable of holding 20 pounds, as long as one did not pick them up . . . or that were built in the shape of a dodecahedron (which was not prohibited). In response to this, the party creating regulations would develop additional prohibitions on these deviant boxes, and the cycle would repeat until the regulations were so lengthy that it would become difficult to determine just exactly what was permitted and desired.

It seems simpler to walk into a restaurant and order what one wants to eat, instead of going in and reading everything on the menu that one does not want. The latter process leaves the cashier, by process of elimination, to figure out what it is that *was not mentioned* and *was thus desired*. Yet when units of government draft land use and building construction regulations, altogether too often they do so by approaching the issue and indicating what is *prohibited* instead of simply saying what they want. If a town is working on appearance standards for a residential community, is it easier to draft text that incorporates all of the requisite elements necessary for approval, or is it easier to include a picture of five elevations that are all acceptable? Taken from the perspective of the homebuilder, is it easier to build houses if a town has five approved elevations, or if there are 20 pages of text indicating what houses *cannot* look like? It should be obvious that if a town has to live with what it orders, it is simpler to say what it is that the town wants, rather than list all of the things it does not want.

Reactionary regulations arose out of uncertainty over the extent to which a governmental entity *could* regulate conduct, coupled with the desire to prohibit excesses that had already happened. Over time, units of government flexed their regulatory muscles, and the courts started to permit an expansion of municipal authorization to tell property owners what they *could and could not* do with their private property.

EUCLIDEAN ZONING: THE BLESSING OF SPECIFIED USES

No discussion of zoning in the United States can be complete without a discussion of the case of *Village of Euclid, Ohio v. Ambler Realty.*[7] Euclid provided a judicial stamp of approval to land use regulations based on the concept of imposing *zoning*, or discrete areas with limited, specified uses, and was such a pivotal decision that this form of zoning has been referred to as Euclidean zoning ever since (with Euclidean referring to the Village, and not to geometry). Euclidean zoning is what most communities are familiar with as a form of land use regulation: land maps covered with colored-in geometrical shape overlays that identify different areas as R-1, B-3, C-5, or otherwise.

In that incredibly significant case, Ambler Realty owned 68 acres in Euclid, a suburb of Cleveland. Under the then-current Euclid zoning

---

7. 272 U.S. 365 (1926).

ordinance that had been adopted in 1922, there were six classes of use, three classes of height, and four area/density classifications. The property owned by Ambler was divided into three use designations. Ambler sought to develop the entirety of the property for industrial use, and in a move that would be unfathomable today, it refused to submit to a hearing before the Village of Euclid zoning board. Even more amazing (from a modern perspective), the trial court sided with Ambler Realty and held that the zoning ordinance was an unconstitutional taking of private property without compensation.

On appeal, the United States Supreme Court determined that the passage of a zoning ordinance was a lawful exercise of the inherent police powers of a municipality. Interestingly, Ambler had offered no substantive evidence that zoning adversely affected property, and the Court thus indicated that it had no basis to determine that Ambler suffered any adverse impact *other than speculation*. One of the most important determinations made in the case was the decision that the standard of review applied in zoning matters is what is called the "rational basis" test. The municipality has to demonstrate that there is some rational basis for its zoning ordinance and supporting regulations. Put another way, the party challenging the zoning ordinance has to prove that the ordinance is discriminatory and has no rational basis. Equally as important, for the first time, the Supreme Court held that there was a *valid governmental interest* in maintaining the character of neighborhoods and in regulating where land uses should occur.

Even as the decision was being rendered, the Supreme Court recognized the significance of the ruling.

> Regulations, the wisdom, necessity and validity of which, as applied to existing conditions, are so apparent that they are now uniformly sustained, a century ago, or even half a century ago, probably would have been rejected as arbitrary and oppressive. Such regulations are sustained, under the complex conditions of our day, for reasons analogous to those which justify traffic regulations, which, before the advent of automobiles and rapid transit street railways, would

have been condemned as fatally arbitrary and unreasonable. And in this there is no inconsistency, for, while the meaning of constitutional guarantees never varies, the scope of their application must expand or contract to meet the new and different conditions which are constantly coming within the field of their operation. In a changing world it is impossible that it should be otherwise. But although a degree of elasticity is thus imparted, not to the meaning, but to the application of constitutional principles, statutes and ordinances, which, after giving due weight to the new conditions, are found clearly not to conform to the Constitution, of course, must fail.

The ordinance now under review, and all similar laws and regulations, must find their justification in some aspect of the police power, asserted for the public welfare. The line which in this field separates the legitimate from the illegitimate assumption of power is not capable of precise delimitation. It varies with circumstances and conditions. A regulatory zoning ordinance, which would be clearly valid as applied to the great cities, might be clearly invalid as applied to rural communities.[8]

With a lawsuit based on the premise that the Village completely lacked the authority to impose a zoning ordinance, the language of the Supreme Court was clear regarding where they believed the authority came from: elected officials.

If the municipal council deemed any of the reasons which have been suggested, or any other substantial reason, a sufficient reason for adopting the ordinance in question, it is not the province of the courts to take issue with the council. We have nothing to do with the question of the wisdom or good policy of municipal ordinances. If they are not satisfying to a majority of the citizens, their recourse is to the ballots—not to the courts.[9]

---

8. 272 U.S. at 386–87.
9. *Id.* at 393.

Now, municipalities across the nation were emboldened by the *Euclid* case to proceed deeper into zoning matters.

▨ STANDARD ZONING AND PLANNING ACTS ▨

In the same year that *Euclid* was decided, the revised Standard State Zoning Enabling Act (SZEA) was released. The original SZEA had been developed in 1924 by an advisory committee on zoning acting under the direction of then Secretary of Commerce Herbert Hoover. Only two years later, the revised SZEA was released, providing another fundamental support for the concept of municipally regulated zoning ordinances.

> For the purpose of promoting health, safety, welfare, morals, or the general welfare of the community, the legislative body of cities and incorporated villages is hereby empowered to regulate and restrict the height, number of stories, and size of buildings and other structures, the percentage of the lot that may be occupied, the size of yards, courts, and other open spaces, the density of population, and the location and use of buildings, structures, and land for trade, industry, residence, or other purposes.[10]

The SZEA advised cities that they were authorized to use planning and zoning authority as a component of their general police powers, without the need for constitutional amendments and without fear of legal repercussions.[11] It laid out proposed standards for different types of zoning districts and concepts of due process for handling zoning applications in a clear and uniform fashion, and formed the foundation for many of the zoning ordinances that were adopted by municipalities thereafter.

---

10. A Standard State Zoning Enabling Act, § 1, Grant of Power (rev. ed. 1926).
11. A Standard State Zoning Enabling Act, Foreword (rev. ed. 1926).

In a period of incredible progress in the area of municipal zoning authority, only two years later (in 1928), the Standard City Planning Enabling Act (SCPEA) was passed in order to encourage municipalities to establish both local planning commissions and master plans for community development (now commonly called Comprehensive Plans). The SCPEA's stated purpose was to do nothing less than revolutionize the field of municipal planning.

> Any municipality is hereby authorized and empowered to make, adopt, amend, extend, add to, or carry out a municipal plan as provided in this act and create by ordinance a planning commission with the powers and duties herein set forth.[12]

Beyond suggesting the creation of the modern Plan Commission, the SCPEA outlined affirmative duties for the SCPEA to undertake forward-looking planning, rather than reactionary regulations.

> It shall be the function and duty of the commission to make and adopt a master plan for the physical development of the municipality, including any areas outside of its boundaries which, in the commission's judgment, bear relation to the planning of such municipality. Such plan, with the accompanying maps, plats, charts and descriptive matter shall show the commission's recommendations for the development of said territory, including, among other things, the general location, character and extent of streets, viaducts, subways, bridges, waterways, water fronts, boulevards, parkways, playgrounds, squares, parks, aviation fields, and other public ways, grounds and open spaces, the general location of public buildings and other public property, and the general location and extent of public utilities and terminals, whether publicly or privately owned or operated, for water, light, sanitation, transportation, communication, power, and other purposes; also the removal, relocation, widening, narrowing, vacating, abandonment, change of use or extension of any of the foregoing ways, grounds, open

---

12.   A Standard City Planning Enabling Act, § 2 (1928).

spaces, buildings, property, utilities, or terminals; as well as a zoning plan for the control of the height, area, bulk, location, and use of buildings and premises.[13]

These three events—the *Euclid* decision, the passage of the amended SZEA, and the passage of the SCPEA—occurred within a two-year period in the 1920s. Within 20 years following these events, 85 percent of all communities in the United States had enacted zoning ordinances with some relation to these events.[14]

Within the same period, two general concepts began to emerge regarding the laws underpinning the authority to zone. First was the concept that zoning had to be based on the rational review/rational basis as described in *Euclid*. Out of their desire to demonstrate rationality, municipalities and state legislatures both undertook to include elements and factors in their zoning ordinances that could be used to evaluate any particular zoning request or the appropriateness of a given zoning designation. These tests sought to create an objective basis to arrive at the conclusion of whether a given zoning designation supported the public health, welfare, safety, and morals (the police powers at the root of the authority to zone).

The second general concept that emerged was a prohibition on the practice known as "contract zoning." Contract zoning is, in the broadest of terms, zoning imposed by agreement between a municipality and a property owner. The property owner could promise any number of benefits to the municipality, including cash, donations, positive benefits, increased revenues, or other consideration, in exchange for receiving a defined, requested zoning designation. The prohibition on contract zoning arose out of a concern by the judiciary that it represented the abandonment of the police powers that gave

---

13. A Standard City Planning Enabling Act, § 6, General Powers and Duties (1928).
14. Oliver Gillham, The Limitless City: A Primer on the Urban Sprawl Debate (2002).

rise to zoning in the first place. If a municipality could impose zoning based on agreement, without regard to the public welfare, zoning would become a business instead of a legislative process.

The prohibition on contract zoning, which became effective on a nearly nationwide basis, produced some unusual results. It might be permissible to approve a commercial development if the "factors" used to evaluate it implied that the public would benefit from the creation of new jobs, additional tax base, and related municipal revenues, but it was impermissible to grant zoning based expressly upon those benefits. Over time, this would be an issue that courts and municipalities alike would struggle with.

▨ ZONING IN THE POSTWAR ERA ▨

As the art of municipal zoning went through its growing pains, the country experienced rapid changes in the post-World War II era. Many zoning commentators relate the growth of zoning ordinances directly to the expansion of transportation. The birth of the railroad, then streetcars, then automobiles, generated a newfound ability for people to travel. No longer would people be forced to live within walking distance of their workplace; now the concept of the commute could be developed. Residential neighborhoods could be built, where residents drove to work in alternate locations. The end of World War II saw GIs returning home, used to motorized transport and demanding suburban housing, roads, and cars.

> Once the war ended, we experienced several decades of unprecedented prosperity, from the mid '40s through the '70s. We built the interstate highway system and moms learned to drive. FHA and VA loans favored single-family homes, primarily new, suburban ones, over denser, multi-family options. We went from single-car families to 2-car families. We embraced the suburban shopping center and the enclosed mall.

Just because it was a whole lot easier, people chose driving themselves over taking public transit. They chose living in the new suburbs over living in established urban areas, especially those that had
experienced decades of deferred maintenance (the Great Depres-
sion followed by wartime rationing). Employers, schools and retail-
ers all responded by offering more and more "free" parking, either
by planning it from the start, in new suburban developments, or by
buying up and tearing down existing buildings in more-established
urban areas. This mobility also resulted in the Euclidean zoning
many of us are questioning today—it codified a preference for con-
venient parking over both density and walkability.

The end result is the world we live in today. It reflects the hopes
and aspirations of the majority of Americans, as reflected by the
actions of our elected officials. We trade sprawl and congested
highways for the "freedom" to live where we want, work where we
can find jobs and to shop at generic chains who have mastered the
worldwide logistics supply chain.[15]

It is a common theme among urban planners to cite the "rise of
the automobile" in the postwar era as the primary reason that suburban sprawl began to take hold. Cheap land, cheap roads, and cheap
gasoline are used as the harbingers of doom for sustainable development and for "walkable" communities. The rise of communities that
are not walkable led to greater dependence on the automobile, which
in turn led to corresponding increases in that critical measurement
of auto use, Vehicle Miles Traveled (VMTs). According to some commentators, nearly all of the evils of "suburbia," ranging from drive-
throughs to obesity, are the necessary by-product of these three items
being available in abundance.

These "evils" of suburbia were fed and enabled by the construction
of massive, nationwide interstate highway projects that were originally
conceived as Cold War defense projects, but which grew into one of

---

15. *Transportation and the Urban Form*, Urban Review STL (Dec. 23, 2009), www
.urbanreviewstl.com/?cat=406.

the most complicated and elaborate roadway systems in the world. The postwar era was a perfect storm of an emerging middle class in the United States, confronting cheap gasoline, expanding roadways, sprawling suburban neighborhoods, and an ease of automotive transportation that had never before been experienced.

One would expect that when any of the raw materials necessary for sprawl increase in price, there would be a corresponding *decrease* in the growth of sprawl, or even a decline in the objective standards available to help measure it. And certainly, when gas prices increase dramatically, there can be short-term decreases in VMTs (nationwide VMTs between January 2007 and January 2008 decreased by some 20 billion miles (out of a total annual average of around 220 billion miles)).[16] But evaluating these mileage trends over longer periods of time—including subsequent periods of high gas prices through 2011,[17] it appears as though decreases in VMT based on higher gasoline prices are temporary trends. This country has become dependent on the automobile and has used zoning and subdivision standards to create automobile-friendly communities for the past century.

For decades, researchers have sought to understand exactly how land use influences VMT. During the 1990's, a number of studies seemed to show that this connection was weak, at best, but these studies suffered from methodology problems and poor data. More recent studies that take advantage of GIS and better data show a stronger link. A landmark 2007 book looked at all the available evidence and concluded that sprawling communities that require car trips to meet most daily needs exhibit 20-40% higher VMT than more compact, mixed-used, and walkable neighborhoods.

---

16. TRAFFIC VOLUME TRENDS, U.S. DEP'T TRANSP., FED. HIGHWAY ADMIN., OFFICE OF HIGHWAY POLICY INFO., http://www.fhwa.dot.gov/policyinformation/ travel_monitoring/tvt.cfm (last visited October 16, 2011).

17. Public Road Mileage Chart; http://www.fhwa.dot.gov/policyinformation/ statistics/2009/vmt421.cfm.

Studies have shown that the following land use and transportation attributes can significantly reduce VMT, by reducing trip lengths, and encouraging alternatives to driving: 1) Placing new development in already developed areas, close to population centers, rather than on the suburban fringe or in exurban (rural) areas; 2) Higher residential densities; 3) Higher retail densities; 4) Connectivity— direct, rather than circuitous, driving and walking connections; 5) A variety of walking-distance destinations, such as groceries, other retail and services, and civic uses; 6) Reduced parking supply, and parking located to the rear of buildings; 7) Frequent, reliable, and comfortable transit service.[18]

So perhaps the reason that a majority of the people in this country are so vehicle-dependent is that the communities people live in force reliance on the personal automobile.

That is not to say that all communities are car-dependent. Some communities have been quite successful in advancing alternative forms of transportation. In suburban areas surrounding large metropolitan centers, the news is constantly replete with smaller municipalities seeking to obtain light rail commuter transportation and other similar mass-transit devices, as those suburbs recognize the increase in property values and the increased draw for potential residents that well-coordinated public transportation can offer. Ironically, these public transportation systems are frequently constructed as "park and ride" systems, where riders drive their cars to the train station, park, and then ride the train to their ultimate destination. Because of the spread of car-dependence, even the process of riding the train requires a car ride first.

There is at least some evidence suggesting that communities offering viable, non-car-dependent, alternative transportation enjoy increased real estate prices and less real estate volatility. In the housing

---

18. *Vehicle Miles Travelled*, Liveable Streets Community, http://streetswiki .wikispaces.com/Vehicle+Miles+Traveled (last visited October 16, 2011).

market collapse between the "peak" market of 2004 and the depressed market of late 2008, three of the most car-dependent communities in the country—Las Vegas, Detroit, and Phoenix—experienced some of the largest declines in property values (–37 percent, –34 percent, and –15 percent respectively), while two real estate markets with the biggest *gain* in prices during a period that otherwise seemed to be a nationwide *decline* were Portland and Seattle (enjoying respective gains of 19 percent and 18 percent), both cities renowned for their alternative transportation systems and pedestrian/bicycle friendliness.

The inherent problem of car-dependent communities is that they become a self-fulfilling prophecy. Once cars become the primary method of transportation in a city, everything must be designed to accommodate cars. Streets become wider, higher driving speeds are allowed, and the city becomes less friendly to pedestrians. Commercial developments become spread out and require substantially more land as they require exorbitant amounts of parking spaces to draw vehicle-bound customers. Distances that are inconsequential in a car become insurmountable on foot, and the process repeats itself.

One hundred years ago, before the car was such an integral part of American life, communities were built as perpendicular grids of intersecting streets that offered immediate, direct pedestrian access to everything within the community. Houses spread out along trolley or train routes, and it was not uncommon to have "mixed-use" downtown areas, where residential housing occupied the upper floors of commercial buildings. The concept of a cul-de-sac was nearly unthinkable; the winding roads and increased walking distances that would result made such planning techniques almost unusable. Looking at many modern suburban communities, it is easy to see where the pre-1940 housing ends and the post-1950 housing begins. Suddenly, the orderly grid of roads gave way to meandering streets with culs-de-sac, and the orderly density of pre-war development turned into strip malls and segregated land uses. Walkability and bikeability decreased in importance, and comprehensive plans focused on a system of arterial streets that could concentrate vehicular traffic instead of gridded streets that inherently separated and filtered traffic.

From a pedestrian standpoint, orderly gridded streets almost always result in shorter walking distances than the winding roads of contemporary suburban subdivisions. Gridded streets rely on dispersion of traffic across a large area to accommodate peak traffic flows and use a comprehensive set of localized traffic control devices (stop signs, street lights, and so forth) to help control the flow of that traffic. When a car or pedestrian encounters traffic in a gridded street area, the traveler is free to simply move over a block and find a route with fewer obstructions, while continuing in the general direction of the destination. Contemporary subdivision design, on the other hand, focuses on creating pods of local roads that drain to collector roads that in turn drain to regional roads. If there is traffic or congestion on a collector or regional road, the traveler finds it difficult, if not impossible, to find an alternate route as the local roads are intentionally designed to avoid creating shortcuts or pass-throughs. And the pedestrian, similarly unable to use local, low-speed roads to walk to a destination, is also funneled to a higher-speed, higher traffic density collector or regional road, with a much more dangerous and less pleasant walking experience. Contemporary suburban street design actively discourages pedestrian traffic and encourages traffic concentration and congestion. In the category of everything old being new again, many communities are finding that a return to gridded streets not only reduces traffic congestion but also encourages walkability and bikeability.

Even with these seemingly insurmountable problems that car dependence has caused, communities are not doomed to an asphalt future. The past 20 years have shown an explosive rebirth of walkable communities and of increased interest in so-called "live/work" spaces that permit much of daily life to occur without turning the ignition key. In addition, with the growth of available technology permitting the linking of centralized and remote offices, "telecommuting" and home offices have increased substantially in popularity. And municipalities find themselves with powerful new tools that can be used to focus and redirect development within.

ANNEXATION AGREEMENTS: A TOOL FOR THE VIRGIN LOT

One of the most powerful tools available in the arsenal of a suburban community is the annexation agreement (also commonly referred to as a development agreement). As its name ("agreement") implies, an annexation agreement is effectively a contract whereby a property owner is permitted to annex to (join) a community in exchange for measured, defined requirements to be met by both sides. Instead of prohibiting contract zoning, courts have encouraged the spread of annexation agreements and have recognized that under such agreements, the "primary consideration" extended to the municipality is the zoning imposed.[19]

Traditional zoning is typically based on an evaluation of "factors and elements" used to justify the imposition of a particular zoning classification. If a community is set up such that it is car-dependent, applying traditional zoning analysis often requires expansive parking and extensive road networks to meet the needs of a public that relies on cars for transportation. Annexation agreements represent one of the tools that communities can use to break this cycle. While there presumably must be some public good underlying the municipality's requirements, through the use of an annexation agreement, a community can impose zoning requirements that can be enforced (usually for a defined period of time) regardless of subsequent changes in needs.

If a community approves a mixed-use development by annexation agreement, and if the developer later decides that it might be cheaper and faster to simply build another residential subdivision, the municipality can hold the developer to their earlier agreement, and

---

19. Langendorf v. City of Urbana, 754 N.E.2d 320 (Ill. 2001).

the developer cannot challenge the zoning based on its revised analysis of the applicable factors. If car-dependence is a factor that forces development to sprawl by virtue of its self-fulfilling prophesy, annexation agreements represent a means of ending that cycle within defined areas (the land subject to the agreement) and giving alternatives an opportunity to catch on and create their own market demand.

"Traditional" zoning mechanisms focus on prohibiting uses that are not wanted instead of focusing on requiring uses that are desired. A property owner develops some idea of what she wants to do with her land and then attempts to get the zoning required to do that. The municipality takes an adverse role, attempting to impose enough restrictions in their zoning code to prevent deleterious uses. With an annexation agreement, the approach can frequently be exactly the opposite; municipalities are often dealing with unimproved areas that represent a blank canvas upon which a wide array of developments are possible.

A brief aside on municipal boundaries and annexations: in many areas, there are multiple municipalities that each desire to expand their boundaries and resulting tax bases and, as a consequence, more than one municipality ends up "competing" to annex the same property. The reason this bears noting is that it completely changes the dynamics of the process of annexing properties. Ordinarily, a municipality contemplating annexing property can accept or reject the annexation and control the terms upon which any property is annexed. When multiple municipalities start competing to annex the same land, the process is inverted. The property owner becomes the one with the control of the negotiations, with municipalities competing to see which one will give more beneficial development terms. These processes quickly become a race to the bottom, where the "winning" municipality that completes the annexation ends up with a project that provides the *developer* with a much better deal than the *municipality* has.

This "race to the bottom" scenario is relevant only to the extent that it precludes municipalities from engaging in thoughtful land planning, and thus is an impediment to sustainable development. When this sort of intergovernmental "competition" can be avoided, both the municipalities and the general public benefit. Depending on the requirements and entitlements of various state laws, some communities might be able to enter into boundary line agreements or other similar intergovernmental agreements, whether formal or informal, to avoid this sort of competition. Anything that can (lawfully) be done to increase the bargaining authority of the municipality in the development negotiations is a step that is more likely to empower a municipality to end up with a plan that it feels is appropriate.

While it is necessary to work with developers in the process of putting together sustainable developments, one must recognize that their objectives might be different from the town's objectives. The vast majority of property developers are for-profit entities, looking to secure permissions, complete a development, make a healthy profit, and then beat a hasty retreat. Long-term involvement with a project, from a developer's perspective, is often five or even ten years; the developer builds a project and then leaves. The municipality lives with the project forever; good or bad, sustainable or not, until it is redeveloped, the project is there to stay. This should make it all the more obvious that a municipality should focus its zoning efforts on prescribing what is desired instead of proscribing a list of things that are not wanted. The act of passing new land use regulations that prohibit specified items can perhaps best be described as creating work for the developers that devote their time to circumventing such regulations.

Returning to the primary subject here, annexation agreements represent a powerful tool for use by municipalities in defining and permitting development that meets their expectations. Because annexation agreements inherently apply to properties that have not been within a municipality before (and thus tend to apply to areas that are either undeveloped or underdeveloped), this tool cannot be wielded to address *every* project. But there are tools that are more flexible in their application and that can be used for a broader range of potential developments.

▓ DEFINING THE FUTURE WITH PLANNED UNIT DEVELOPMENTS ▓

One such tool is the Planned Unit Development or PUD. While their characteristics vary from state to state, generally speaking, a PUD is a means of providing for alternative zoning and development standards within a geographically defined area. A PUD can involve a single lot or thousands of acres; it can apply to residential, commercial, or industrial development. PUDs can incorporate deviations from ordinary zoning requirements that would ordinarily require a variation or special use, or that would otherwise be outright prohibited. With specific respect to *sustainable* development, a PUD can be incredibly useful.

> Most planned unit development (PUD) local laws seek to achieve greater design flexibility and economies of scale in the development of particular land areas within the community. Above all, PUD provisions target specific goals and objectives included in the municipality's comprehensive plan. Generally, PUD local laws anticipate projects that develop a tract of land as a unit (relatively large scale, but not always) in a unified manner.[20]

A PUD can be narrowly tailored to unique, local circumstances and the specific characteristics of any given property that is contemplated for development. They can accommodate new construction, old construction, and reconstruction of nearly any property.

> PUDs are among the most flexible of zoning techniques because their provisions are set by local law. Whereas standard zoning may promote lot-by-lot development in which the entire tract is covered with lots of uniform size, PUD local laws can include the possibility of several medium-sized or smaller lots where the owners work together in using the PUD development options provided by the community. PUDs also provide the opportunity to achieve flexibil-

---

20. *A Guide to Planned Unit Development*, NYS Legislative Committee on Rural Resources, Fall 2005, http://www.dos.state.ny.us/lg/publications/Planned Unit Development Guide.pdf (last visited October 16, 2011).

ity in architectural design, a mix of compatible land uses as well as the preservation of key natural or historic features, that are otherwise difficult to achieve using traditional, lot-by-lot zoning.[21]

The risks of PUDs must also be considered. They are incredibly flexible and can be tailored to many situations. That inherent flexibility is also the greatest potential problem with a PUD.

A PUD can be based on approval of a specified plan (e.g., "approval of the concept plan dated XX.XX.XX and all zoning permissions, variances, special uses and other deviations from the Zoning Code of the Village of _____ as shall be necessary to permit development in accordance therewith"), or it can be based on textual descriptions that simply replace traditional zoning requirements with alternate standards. Because the PUD can be used to almost completely obviate the need to comply with other zoning and development standards, a poorly defined PUD can simply be a license for a developer to construct a sub-par project. In other words, PUDs are great tools because they permit a community to demand and obtain exactly what it is looking for. But for this process to work, the community *has to know what it is looking for, and has to be able to translate that knowledge into specific, tangible standards, plans, or schematics.* If PUDs enable communities to host developments that answer to a higher calling, the community must be able to define what the goals for the PUD are. The Zoning Code for the City of Gurnee, Illinois, is a prime example of a municipality defining what the PUD's goals are.

> The purpose of Planned Unit Development regulations is to encourage and allow more creative and imaginative design of land developments than is possible under district zoning regulations. Planned Unit Development is intended to allow substantial flexibility in planning and designing a proposal. This flexibility often accrues in the form of relief from compliance with conventional zoning ordinance site and design requirements. Ideally, this flexibility results

---

21. *Id.*

in a development that is better planned, that contains more amenities, and ultimately a development that is more desirable to live in than one produced in accordance with typical zoning ordinance and subdivision controls. An intrinsic, and often neglected, premise upon which the approval of a Planned Unit Development (PUD) must be conditioned, is that while greater density or more lenient siting requirements may be granted, the Planned Unit Development should contain features not normally required of traditional developments. Inherent to realizing these objectives, is continuous and in-depth scrutiny of the proposed Planned Unit Development is being adhered to. Hence, to enable thorough analysis of a Planned Unit Development, more information is demanded about the proposal than would be required if development were being pursued under conventional zoning requirements.[22]

That section of municipal code says much about the PUD—it has great promise, and with that promise comes great responsibility. Because of the *flexibility* of a PUD, it often requires greater scrutiny and review and requires a focus on what the underlying goals of the municipality are. Gurnee goes on to define their goals as follows:

Through proper planning and design, each Planned Unit Development should include features which further, and are in compliance with, the following objectives:

1. To allow for the design of developments that are architecturally and environmentally innovative, and that achieve better utilization of land than is possible through strict application of standard zoning and subdivision controls.
2. To encourage land development that, to the greatest extent possible, preserves natural vegetation, respects natural topographic and geologic conditions, and refrains from adversely affective flooding, soil, drainage, and other natural ecologic conditions.

22. City Code for City of Gurnee, Illinois, Chapter 9, Section 9.0, Purpose. http://www.gurnee.il.us/community_dev/zoning_ordinance/09#9.0 (last visited October 16, 2011).

3. To combine and coordinate architectural styles, building forms, and structural/visual relationships within an environment that allows mixing of different land uses in an innovative and functionally efficient manner.

4. To provide for abundant, accessible, and property located public open and recreation space, private open and recreation space, schools, and other public and private facilities.

5. To promote the efficient use of land resulting in networks of utilities, streets and other infrastructure features that maximize the allocation of fiscal and natural resources.

6. To enable land developments to be completely compatible and congruous with adjacent and nearby land developments.

7. To ensure that development occurs at proper locations, away from environmentally sensitive areas, and on land physically suited to construction.

8. To allow unique and unusual land uses to be planned for and located in a manner that ensures harmony with the surrounding community.

9. To create a method for the permanent preservation of historic buildings and/or landmarks.[23]

As discussed above, traditional zoning requires evaluation of a series of factors that have either been defined by a state legislature or a group of judges. The PUD ordinance allows a community to define the factors and elements that are analyzed in the PUD review process based on local needs and values.

Adopting a PUD ordinance or permitting a parcel of land to be developed as a PUD does not necessarily mean that the development will be designed as or will function as a "sustainable" development. But if sustainable development is the stated goal of a community, a PUD ordinance allows that community to develop a zoning process that rewards elements of sustainable development. Instead of a

---

23. City Code for City of Gurnee, Illinois, Chapter 9, Section 9.1, Goals. http://www.gurnee.il.us/community_dev/zoning_ordinance/09#9.1 (last visited October 16, 2011).

"traditional" suburban development with blocks of R-1/R-2 single/ multifamily housing that are serviced by a segregated C-1 commercial strip mall and a small office/research (OR) corridor (and, of course, some carefully isolated industrial uses), all of which encourage dependence on cars and reduce the walkability of a community, a PUD ordinance can reward mixed-use development with comparatively higher residential densities that are interspersed between and within attractive commercial and office mixed-use buildings.

A PUD is not a panacea; a municipality cannot adopt a PUD ordinance and thereafter expect every issue to be magically resolved. But if goals are or can be identified, the PUD is a means of introducing flexibility into ordinarily rigid zoning regulations to permit diverse development and to reward ingenuity. Also, PUDs can be used to approve a specific drawing or plan for development. Instead of approving a set of numerical and text-based zoning prohibitions, a PUD can enable a municipality to get exactly what they see. A plan can be developed for one specific area, and the PUD can approve that plan based on unique, local characteristics. In law school, students are told about a famous U.S. Supreme Court case where a Justice was having a difficult time defining exactly what constituted pornography; his ultimate retort was, "I know it when I see it." Municipal officials often have the same problem defining, in a zoning ordinance, what exactly constitutes "good development." Seeing the proposal and being able to approve, through the PUD process, a map and picture showing exactly what it will look like enables communities to simply say that they know good development when they see it. The PUD allows narrowly tailored permissions for one specific area of land and incorporates great flexibility for that development.

But what becomes of the municipal zoning ordinance when PUDs are used? Certainly, a PUD can be used for many projects, but the level of detail and review inherent in the PUD process renders it cost prohibitive for small-scale development. Moreover, it would almost certainly be prohibited to have a zoning code that *only permits PUD development*, without any underlying or alternative zoning classifications for existing areas of a community. The PUD process requires some level of agreement and cooperation between property owner and municipal regulator; as that cooperation cannot always be assumed to exist, some sort of alternative zoning requirements must be in place.

▒ EVERYTHING OLD IS NEW AGAIN: THE FORM-BASED CODE ▒

A PUD enables a community to look at one specific project and tailor the development requirements to that project; one of their unique strengths is that, in many instances, a town can "see" the finished project before the first shovel of dirt is moved. Form-based codes are a way of developing zoning standards that permit this sort of "visual" approach to a community-wide zoning code. In the simplest of terms, form-based codes deviate from "traditional" zoning ordinances in two primary ways: (1) they focus more on building aesthetics, form, relationships, and characteristics than permitted or prohibited uses; and (2) they emphasize use of drawings and schematics in lieu of textual descriptions. According to the Form-Based Codes Institute (FBCI), form-based codes "foster predictable built results and a high-quality public realm by using physical form (rather than separation of uses) as the organizing principle for the code. . . . Form-based codes address the relationship between building facades and the public realm, the form and mass of buildings in relation to one another, and the scale and types of streets and blocks."[24]

Conventional zoning focuses on regulatory prohibitions. Efforts to produce a regulation that generates only desired development has resulted in the generation of zoning ordinances that are dense, hard to understand, and pervasive in their regulatory scheme. A traditional zoning ordinance will result in segregation of uses and will regulate

---

24. FORM-BASED CODES INSTITUTE, DEFINITION OF A FORM-BASED CODE, http://www.formbasedcodes.org/what-are-form-based-codes (last visited Oct. 11, 2011).

based on the imposition of requirements that must be satisfied (set-back distances, floor-area ratios, etc.). Form-based codes, on the other hand, are offered as a means of zoning by providing examples of the *desired* development outcome (representations of what is permitted instead of prohibitions on what *is not* permitted), and true form-based codes rely on the building form to serve as an inherent limitation on what the resulting uses of the underlying property can be.

Form-based codes frequently include a number of elements that would be customary in a "traditional" zoning code and a number of elements that would be foreign to Euclidean zoning practitioners. Those elements include the following:

Regulating Plan. A plan or map of the regulated area designating the locations where different building form standards apply, based on clear community intentions regarding the physical character of the area being coded.

Public Space Standards. Specifications for the elements within the public realm (e.g., sidewalks, travel lanes, on-street parking, street trees, street furniture, etc.).

Building Form Standards. Regulations controlling the configuration, features, and functions of buildings that define and shape the public realm.

Administration. A clearly defined application and project review process.

Definitions. A glossary to ensure the precise use of technical terms.

Architectural Standards. Regulations controlling external architectural materials and quality.

Landscaping Standards. Regulations controlling landscape design and plant materials on private property as they impact public spaces (e.g., regulations about parking lot screening and shading, maintaining sight lines, insuring unobstructed pedestrian movements, etc.).

Signage Standards. Regulations controlling allowable signage sizes, materials, illumination, and placement.

Environmental Resource Standards. Regulations controlling issues such as storm water drainage and infiltration, development on slopes, tree protection, solar access, etc.

Annotation. Text and illustrations explaining the intentions of specific code provisions.[25]

Interestingly, a community's development ordinances might include all of these elements and *still not be considered a form-based code by the FBCI.* This is because the FBCI believes that the criteria used to identify form-based codes include the questions of whether the code is enforceable, easy to use, and whether it will produce functional and vital urbanism.[26] Thus, a code that is form-based but not user-friendly would not qualify as a form-based code, and a code that is otherwise form-based but that produces a rural aesthetic is not a form-based code (at least in the eyes of the FBCI).

The FBCI is certainly one of the leaders in the area of form-based coding and so-called "new urbanism," and expends a significant amount of its energy encouraging community planners to adopt form-based codes. Peter Katz, president of the FBCI, has penned an article listing what he believes to be the eight primary benefits of form-based codes, which can be summarized as follows:

1. They are prescriptive rather than proscriptive, which adds predictability to the outcome of any development.
2. They encourage public participation by allowing citizens to see the consequences of changes in the zoning code.
3. They permit orderly, predictable development on any scale (large or small).
4. They result in the construction of projects that are diverse in architecture, materials, uses, and ownership.

---

25. *Id.*
26. FORM-BASED CODES INSTITUTE, CHECKLIST FOR IDENTIFYING AND EVALUATING FORM BASED CODES, http://www.formbasedcodes.org/take-quiz (last visited Oct. 11, 2011).

5. They can be adapted to codify existing community identities and thus work well in established neighborhoods.

6. The visual nature of form-based codes makes them easier for nonprofessionals to use, and makes it easier to determine if a given development conforms to the applicable requirements.

7. They eliminate the need for wordy text descriptions of the desired outcome and eliminate the need for extensive subjective review by governing bodies, resulting in more predictable, and potentially less expensive, development review.

8. They may be more enforceable than traditional zoning requirements that include design guidelines (at least in already developed areas) because they replace subjectivity in design restrictions with the generation of "forms" and spaces that are designed to promote public health, welfare, and safety.[27]

If those are truly the benefits of form-based codes, then it would seem as though every community would be rushing out to replace antiquated zoning ordinances with form-based codes that promote all of these virtues.

However, one of the chief criticisms that can be leveled at some advocates of form-based coding is the insistence that a development ordinance is only a form-based code if it promotes new urbanism. If a development ordinance is otherwise "form-based" but produces a non-urban result, the FBCI might not consider it to be form-based. (Of course, form-based codes assume that there will still be less intensive uses in some areas, and focus upon the creation of a multitude of different forms). But some communities have been unwilling to completely give up the tenets of Euclidean zoning in favor of the freer-flowing aesthetic of form-based codes. Often, these communities try to incorporate some elements of form-based codes (e.g., pictures and

---

27. Peter Katz, former president, FORM-BASED CODES INSTITUTE, EIGHT ADVANTAGES TO FORM-BASED CODES, *available at* http://tampafl.gov/dept_Land_Development/files/Eight_Advantages_to_Form.pdf (last visited Oct. 11, 2011).

graphics instead of textual descriptions) with some elements of traditional zoning codes (e.g., parking requirements, building setback lines, anti-monotony provisions). These hybrid zoning codes are an attempt to gather some of the benefits of form-based coding without giving up all of the control of "traditional" zoning.

As might be expected, advocates of form-based codes do not necessarily smile upon these hybrid codes.

> Because the form standards are not fully developed in such hybrid codes, hyper-control of uses continues. Changes in market cycle require constant legislative changes to the zoning regulations. The lack of precise standards diminishes the predictability of the outcome. Discretionary review continues. The uncertainty is played out at individual project levels in contentious and protracted public hearings.[28]

The reason for this concern is understandable. Form-based codes were intended to be the cure for wordy, burdensome, and unduly restrictive zoning ordinances. By shifting the focus away from the *use* and to the *form*, the aesthetically pleasing result was ensured. Moreover, from a practical perspective, if the form is adequately defined, the reasonable uses of a building will be functionally restricted. A concrete crushing plant simply cannot locate itself within a three-story mixed-use contemporary development.

However, from the perspective of a municipal attorney or elected town official, the reluctance to completely eliminate use restrictions and similar controls is understandable. While a concrete crushing plant cannot locate itself within the building described above, a tattoo parlor, strip club, or other use that is commonly viewed as "deleterious" certainly could locate in the building.

Form-based coding advocates often compare two proposed streetscapes that are possible under different zoning ordinances. The

---

28. Kaizer Rangwala, *Hybrid Codes versus Form-Based Codes*, NEW URBAN NEWS, April/May 2009, at 12.

"traditional" zoning ordinance example is always, without fail, unattractive, incongruous, and poorly designed. The "form-based" example will have pleasant architecture, tree-lined streets, and a more pedestrian-friendly perspective. These sorts of comparisons are not entirely fair. If a city with a "traditional" zoning ordinance sought to produce pleasant, tree-lined boulevards, they could do so with appropriate textual restrictions. But the benefits of form-based coding (simplified ordinances, certain outcomes, aesthetic benefits) are many, and if a community can agree on a visual objective, that objective will almost certainly be easier to define with *form-based* regulations than textual regulations. Purist objections aside, however, there is no reason that a form-based code cannot incorporate appropriate textual restrictions on uses and other matters that are important to elected officials (and their constituents). Form-based codes can have a number of advantages over traditional ordinances—and, at the very least, the ability to prescribe the "look" of approved development. There is no practical reason that a community cannot use form-based codes for their many benefits but couple those benefits with practical, textual restrictions that ensure the new, attractive buildings will not be filled with new, unattractive businesses.

THE TRANSECT: HOW REALISTIC IS YOUR VISION?

In its most basic terms, the "transect" is the idea of using land use restrictions to create a continuum of zoning from least intensive uses (park, open space, natural habitat) to the most intensive uses (urban, industrial, etc.).[29] Transects are not a concept that are limited to zoning ordinances.

> A transect is a cut or path through part of the environment showing a range of different habitats. Biologists and ecologists use tran-

---

29. A good, visual example of the transect appears at http://www.transect.org/rural_img.html.

sects to study the many symbiotic elements that contribute to habitats where certain plants and animals thrive. Human beings also thrive in different habitats. Some people prefer urban centers and would suffer in a rural place, while others thrive in the rural or sub-urban zones. Before the automobile, American development patterns were walkable, and transects within towns and city neighborhoods revealed areas that were less urban and more urban in character. This urbanism could be analyzed as natural transects are analyzed. To systemize the analysis and coding of traditional patterns, a prototypical American rural-to-urban transect has been divided into six Transect Zones, or T-zones, for application on zoning maps. This zoning system replaces conventional separated-use zoning systems that have encouraged a car-dependent culture and land-consuming sprawl. The six Transect Zones instead provide the basis for real neighborhood structure, which requires walkable streets, mixed use, transportation options, and housing diversity. The T-zones vary by the ratio and level of intensity of their natural, built, and social components. They may be coordinated to all scales of planning, from the region through the community scale down to the individual lot and building. The new zoning itself is applied at the community (municipal) scale.[30]

According to the Center for Applied Transect Studies, the concept can be applied to any community.

> Codes and architectural pattern books based on the Transect must be calibrated for each place, to reflect local character and form. Depending on the place, there may be fewer or more T-zones determined by analysis. For example, most towns do not have a T-6 Urban Core Zone.[31]

That last comment is a bit of an understatement. Many communities, depending on their size and location, will only have two or

---

30. CENTER FOR APPLIED TRANSECT STUDIES, THE TRANSECT, http://www.transect .org/transect.html (last visited Apr. 15, 2010).

31. *Id.*

three of the distinctly defined transects within their boundaries. Extremely rural communities will not reach the greater densities of one extreme of the transect, and while extremely urban communities might have open space and parks, they will not likely have a continuum of gradually decreasing densities leading up to those open spaces.

One of the common issues with implementing form-based codes within smaller communities (or within a small area of a larger community) is the issue of defining transects. Frankly, it is impossible to go from a T-1 to a T-6 transect within the confines of a four-block development. For that reason, a form-based code being adopted for a four-block-sized development does not need to define all six transects; including such definitions unnecessarily complicates the zoning code. And yet, some planners believe that a form-based code has to include all transects in order to be complete. From a practical perspective, returning to the goal-based analysis described in the introduction of this book, if the goal is to have a simple, enforceable, readily useable development code, that code should be as uncomplicated as possible and should not include extraneous regulations or descriptions of zoning areas or transects that could never be included or constructed within the regulated properties. A rural community that will never have T-6 ultra-urban areas within its confines does itself a disservice when it adopts a form-based code that includes regulations relating to T-6 transects, just as an urban city with no agricultural area does itself a disservice when it reverses that error by regulating agricultural areas that do not exist.

There is still merit to the concept of the transect, whatever form of zoning regulations it is applied to. When applied to property *use*, the transect permits gradually increasing intensity of use and encourages the location of compatible uses in adjacent areas. It also encourages commercial development by permitting greater concentrations of businesses in areas that have greater concentrations of population. Corresponding transportation efficiencies (reducing VMTs by locating dense population near dense employment and services) can be achieved, and other similar benefits can be obtained.

The ideal purpose of the transect is simple and practical: permit gradual and orderly transitions between uses and densities. If drawing a community from a blank slate, it would be easy to draw a map that shows such gradual transitions. In dealing with existing communities and redevelopment matters, it can be more difficult to adhere to. There are practical reasons for deviating from the transect from time to time and permitting distinct uses to be adjoining. For example, few would argue that Central Park in New York City should be paved over and developed as high-intensity commercial/residential development in accordance with the usage of surrounding parcels. But, when planning from a theoretical perspective, and when determining how to create zoning standards that will work—and creating use distinctions that are realistic and enforceable—the concept of transitioning between varying uses and separating incompatible uses with *physical* separation is one that is sensible.

On a brief historical note, transects can be taken too far, as well. The postwar drive to build suburban bliss often included locating industrial and commercial businesses and other similar places of employment in areas where they were distant from residential subdivisions. Serving the goal of providing suburban residential experiences and keeping the noise and bustle of industrial uses away from homes seems like a sensible idea. However, when this idea gets pushed too far, it results in people living lives where their place of residence is distant from their place of employment—and again forces a dependence on cars for transportation. Certainly, not all places of employment can be located adjacent to housing; no one wants to live next to a concrete crushing plant. But where possible, integrating living and working spaces, or at least minimizing the distances between them (and serving those distances with bicycle lanes and public transportation) can make dramatic inroads toward supporting sustainable practices.

▨ QUESTION EVERYTHING YOU KNOW:
PARKING, WALKING, AND RIDING ▨

Sustainable development advocates often talk about incorporating mass transit into designs and ensuring that developments interface well with bus, rail, and other similar transportation. Mass transit is great where it is available, but the hard reality is that not every community has light rail or even bus service available. And while every suburb and collar community would love to attract a train station, even where light rail is available, a stop might not be conveniently located for local riders. So as communities develop new planning and zoning codes and ordinances, while incorporating public transportation is great, communities must also plan for those parts of transportation that they can accommodate.

For all of the criticism of shopping malls (which usually incorporate huge amounts of imperviously paved parking areas surrounding them), they do have one clear and rarely recognized benefit: malls are almost always park-once environments. People who go to the mall park and go into the mall, walk to multiple stores, and then walk back to their cars. As malls expand into surrounding strip malls and retail fronting main streets, that "park-once" mentality is lost. And as malls are replaced by "lifestyle centers," often consisting of nothing more than dolled-up strip centers, the park-once mentality is impossible.

For the past 60 years, communities have looked at development and imposed *minimum* parking requirements. They identify each use and require each use to provide its own parking. They prevent commercial development from occurring in some areas because landowners cannot meet the minimum parking requirements. Think about this issue practically. Who has a bigger incentive to want to be easily accessible to customers: the retailer or the municipality? If a retailer is willing to locate in a given area, and if they think the parking will be adequate, are arbitrary parking standards something that should be enforced to preclude development? There is a significant amount of emerging planning scholarship suggesting that "minimum" parking requirements are counterproductive and should be replaced with "maximum" parking requirements that cannot be exceeded. Including too much parking generates unnecessary storm water runoff, creates too much separation between uses (again making walkability difficult), and converts what could be sales and property tax-generating developable space into unattractive oases of asphalt.

As maximum and minimum parking requirements are considered, the other consideration that is almost always lost in the shuffle is the *location* of parking. One of the most effective ways of reducing VMTs and increasing pedestrian traffic is creating environments that are conducive to the "park-once" mentality. Municipalities can create areas that have readily available parking in centralized locations, surrounded by very walkable commercial districts. Uses can be located so as to be appropriately spaced from the parking lots. Some uses (e.g., dry cleaners) should be located closer to parking so as to permit large bundles of clothes to be carried back to cars. Some uses can be located farther from parking without deleterious effects. Instead of allocating X number of parking spots per square foot of commercial area and requiring on-site parking, sustainable planning requires creating environments that minimize the importance of and need for cars, and maximizes the ability of people to feel safe when walking. It requires creating developments that are dense enough to have a variety of shops within a reasonable walking radius. It requires reevaluating many of the requirements that are otherwise reflexively enforced against developments.

Is it more beneficial to have consumers drive to a mall, park once, and walk from store to store in an environment where the lighting, security, HVAC, and other resources are shared in a high-density environment, or is it more beneficial to have a "lifestyle center" where customers park at one end, visit one store, walk back outside to their cars, drive partway down the center, park again, visit a second store, and repeat the cycle? Lifestyle centers organized as long strip centers discourage pedestrian and bicycle traffic by increasing the distance between destinations and by comingling vehicular and pedestrian traffic. If a shopping "center" must be constructed, a community look-ing to support sustainable development should look at creating a park-once environment, where walkability between stores is encouraged and return trips to cars are discouraged. Even better, the shopping center should be pedestrian- and bicycle-accessible and accessible by public transportation to reduce the need for parking at all.

One other note on the unexpected benefits of walkable environ-ments—this is a benefit that can be personally experienced through a little social experiment. One can find a nearby community with a walkable commercial district. One can then drive through the dis-trict, trying to window shop while driving. Then, the same person can walk the district and window shop. Which experience is more likely to cause the consumer to see the wares and merchandise for sale in the district? Is it easier to pop into a store without advanced planning if one is driving, or walking? Walking slows down consumer traffic and increases the chances for window shopping and sales tax generation. It makes it possible to stop in any store to browse without needing to circle the block and look for parking.

The pedestrian-friendly, walkable environments are those that are most effective at generating sales and related revenue, and are the most effective long-term commercial districts. In many instances, these walkable areas are historic areas of communities, where the development predated the automobile—and as a practical conse-quence of that fact, the areas are oriented toward mass transit and pedestrian traffic. One of the great ironies of the rise of the automo-bile and the resulting desire of municipalities to cater to the parking needs of a car-centric society is that it has resulted in far less efficient use of land and generates a self-fulfilling prophecy. Huge parking lots preclude walking and produce more huge parking lots. Looking at historical, established commercial developments that did not accom-modate cars because cars did not exist often provides a guidebook to developing property in a sustainable, pedestrian-friendly fashion.

A note should be included about bicycles as well. Many communi-ties stress the importance of "multiple use trails" (MUT) or "walking and biking trails." These combined-use trails may have their place, but their limitations must also be understood. First, in the case of serious cyclists who are avid riders, designing a biking trail that will accommodate their use will be incredibly difficult. Avid road cyclists travel at speeds that render pedestrian trails unsafe, and that render repeated curb crossings and other similar impediments dangerous. Many a confused municipal planner has looked at a cyclist riding down the street *next to a bike path*, and wondered why the path is not in use. The simple reason is that at 20 or more miles per hour, a road cyclist simply cannot function on an MUT.

Separate from avid road cyclists, the difficulties of combining pedestrian and bicycle traffic in one confined area should be considered by any municipality that desires to build an infrastructure that serves more than just cars. Even a very casual cyclist can pedal along relatively easily at ten miles per hour—which is nearly triple the average walking speed that planners contemplate for pedestrian travel. Frankly, cyclists and walkers often impede each other's travel. In an ideal layout, planners would create a narrower walkway on one side of the street and a wider, delineated bike lane or path on the other side (or integrated into the street itself) to accommodate both forms of travel.

European cities have been designed with bicycles in mind for over a century; their obesity rates reflect the greater emphasis on pedal-powered transportation as compared with the United States' car-centric waistlines. Designing a community that permits and encourages bicycle use is not only environmentally friendly, but it also builds a different form of consumer traffic flow to local businesses and attracts people that are interested in a healthy, vibrant area. In this book, there is much discussion of car parking. As a community ponders bicycle use, it must also consider bicycle parking. Providing a secure, well-lit, preferably covered area for cyclists to ride to and lock up their bicycles is paramount in attracting and retaining bicycle-based commuting, shopping, and tourism. It is no accident that bicycle-friendly towns have shown better property value retention than car-centric communities. There are a multitude of bike lane design studies, forms and models available for communities that seek to start taking the first steps towards a bike-friendly transportation infrastructure; the City of Chicago has promulgated one such model which covers a wide array of potential designs and their attributes.[32]

Understanding both the history of zoning and the arsenal of modern planning tools available to communities (many of which are the modern implementations of historical concepts) can help improve the quality of any set of land use regulations that a municipality uses and can enable public agencies to work toward meeting any goal. If the goal is working toward more sustainable development, the concepts described above (development agreements, PUDs, form-based coding, transects) can be crafted in such a way as to both *require* and *reward* sustainability. Developers frequently want to build higher densities than municipalities desire; the developers want to build taller and on a larger scale than the public officials initially are comfortable with. Developers want to build both the rooftops and the resulting commercial space; these goals can benefit local governments as well, if planned appropriately.

Careful implementation of these planning tools can permit developers to achieve these profit-driven goals while creating attractive, high-quality developments. Elected officials and concerned members of the public both feel more comfortable with higher density developments when they can (1) control the result (development agreements), (2) visualize the end result (form-based codes), (3) see how the development fits within the continuum of uses needed in the community (transect), and (4) relate present development to past successes and model communities that they desire to emulate. The land use regulations create the potential for development (and the building standards, engineering projects, and other natural products thereof). More than anything else, the land use regulations set the stage for success, or they doom a community to boredom and to clichés of suburbia.

---

32. CHICAGO BIKE LANE DESIGN GUIDE. http://www.activelivingresources.org/assets/chicagobikelanedesignguide.pdf (last accessed 10/17/11).

3

Engineering a Sustainable Community

Many of the technical specifications of the items to be discussed in this book require assistance from a civil engineer licensed to practice in the local jurisdiction. The general reluctance that many public officials have to exploring and gaining at least a *basic* understanding of some of the technologies available to handle modern development in a sustainable fashion has to be addressed. Just as some lawyers believe they can benefit by drawing up a contract that can only be understood by a lawyer, for many years, engineers have developed plans and engineered projects in such a fashion as to make the underlying scientific concepts incorporated into those projects opaque and immune to lay understanding.

Part of the obligation of anyone contemplating sustainable development is to gain a basic understanding of the mechanisms by which utility and infrastructure services are provided. That is true from both a public official and private developer perspective. Civil engineering, in many respects, addresses the most basic needs of communities: those needs include fresh water, sanitary conditions, infrastructure for regular (and emergency) transportation, and gas/electrical services for heating, lighting, and a host of other uses. For many years, the goal of communities was to reap the most benefits possible from the surrounding environment. Water sources were drilled and pumped, waste was discharged into streams to be carried away, and forests and open spaces were paved for highways. For a host of reasons, communities are increasingly looking at ways of being more environmentally conscious with their development decisions, and are including new technologies to minimize and mitigate the environmental consequences of development.

Engineering a sustainable community still requires the expertise of trained professionals, but there is much that a concerned member of the public or an interested public official can do to educate herself about these issues. What follows is a discussion and exploration, in general terms, of the past, present, and future of civil engineering topics that municipalities need to understand in order to better regulate development and implement sensible requirements for new construction.

WASTEWATER: HARMLESS BY-PRODUCT, TOXIC WASTE, OR RENEWABLE RESOURCE?

Wastewater is something that has been viewed for centuries as a problem to mitigate rather than a resource to manage. Step back from suburbia and consider a camping trip in a national park. When selecting a location to pitch a tent, would a camper place the tent in a large gully that obviously serves as a storm water drainageway? Would she place it on an eroded hillside that shows evidence of significant natural storm water flows? Obviously, when picking a spot to pitch a tent, people naturally look for locations that have good drainage and that will not subject them to a huge infiltration of rainwater in the event of a passing storm.

But when communities move beyond tents and start constructing houses, offices, and commercial developments, the concern for avoiding obvious drainage issues is seemingly replaced with a notion that we can engineer our way out of nearly any issue. Whatever the drainage challenge that may be presented, a big enough ditch, detention pond, or other storm water management technique can drain away that water and keep our developments safe. This approach is not without problems. "Traditional stormwater management has been to convey runoff in storm sewers to detention basins, and onto the natural drainage way. Sediment and pollutants can be carried along with the runoff and ultimately end up in rivers and streams."[1] If the goal of traditional storm water management is to prevent flooding by carrying rainwater to nearby watercourses, the consequences of failing to properly manage storm water (and recognize its impacts on other municipal utilities such as sanitary sewage) have been clear for a long time.

> In 1885, a severe rainstorm caused sewage-contaminated river water to flow into Lake Michigan, contaminating the City [of Chicago's] drinking water. This disaster led to a cholera and typhoid outbreak that killed over 90,000 people. Repeated outbreaks of epidemic diseases compelled the City to find a way to stop the flow of polluted [storm water] into Lake Michigan.[2]

The earliest attempts at managing storm water focused on integrating storm water into the emerging technology of sanitary sewer systems, thus creating what is commonly referred to as a Combined Sewer System (CSS). "CSSs are wastewater collection systems designed to carry sanitary sewage (consisting of domestic, commercial and industrial wastewater) and stormwater (surface drainage from rainfall or snowmelt) in a single pipe to a treatment facility."[3] The obvious consequence of a CSS is that every drop of water conveyed, whether storm water or raw sewage, has to run through a wastewater treatment plant (WWTP) (thus greatly expanding the volume of water that must be accommodated by such plants). The inefficiency of such a system is

---

1. Jeremy C. Lin & Dean M. Frieders, *The Future of Stormwater Management: Bioswales and Environmentally Friendly Stormwater Control, Part I*, ILL. MUN. LEAGUE REV., Oct. 2008, at 17.
2. Suzanne Malec, City of Chicago Dep't of Env't, *Storm Water Management in the City of Chicago*, http://www.epa.gov/nps/natlstormwater03/21Malec.pdf (last visited Mar. 4, 2010).
3. CSSs Combined Sewer Overflows: Guidance for Nine Minimum Conditions, at 1-1, EPA Document No. 832-B-95-003, May 1995.

clear: every drop of wastewater conveyed through the CSS has to undergo the same, most intensive treatment in order to render the discharge "safe." Storm water that may have no or minimal pollutant value is treated in the same fashion as the most polluted sewage or industrial wastewater. Even with that significant cost disadvantage, CSSs serve tens of millions of people within the United States alone and are used in literally thousands of US cities, including cities as large as Portland, Oregon.[4]

One unfortunate consequence of CSSs is that they have the capacity to generate peak flows during large storms that greatly exceed the available treatment capacity of WWTPs. The unintended consequence of CSSs is the phenomenon of the Combined Sewer Overflow (CSO), a bypass mechanism that is intentionally engineered into CSSs to permit excess storm flows to be discharged without treatment (but after having been comingled with raw sewage).

> Combined Sewer Overflows are typically found in older cities. These systems were designed to collect rainwater runoff, domestic sewage, and industrial rainwater all in the same pipe. Most of the time, combined sewer systems transport all of their wastewater to a sewage treatment plant. However, during periods of heavy rainfall or melting snow the volume of wastewater going into the pipes can exceed the capacity and excess wastewater empties directly into nearby streams, rivers or other water bodies.[5]

According to the United States Environmental Protection Agency (USEPA), CSSs are responsible for the discharge of roughly 11.5 trillion gallons of treated wastewater per year, 850 billion gallons of *untreated* CSO (i.e., combined storm water and sewage) per year, and an additional 3 to 10 billion gallons of *untreated raw sewage* per year.[6]

---

4. *Id.*
5. *Combined Sewer Overflows*, www.epa.gov/reg3wapd/cso/index.htm (last visited Feb. 13, 2010).
6. Executive Summary of the Report to Congress on the Impacts and Control of CSOs and SSOs, at ES-7.

For communities that operate CSSs, the EPA has developed what have been dubbed the "Nine Minimum Controls" that are now applicable to their operation. Those include:

1. Proper operation and regular maintenance programs for the sewer system and CSO outfalls.
2. Maximum use of the collection system for storage.
3. Review and modification of pretreatment requirements to ensure that CSO impacts are minimized.
4. Maximization of flow to the publicly owned water treatment facility for treatment of CSS flows.
5. Elimination of CSOs during dry weather and normal conditions.
6. Control of solid and floatable materials in CSOs.
7. Pollution prevention programs to reduce contaminants in CSOs.
8. Public notification to ensure that the public receives adequate notification of CSO occurrences and CSO impacts.
9. Monitoring to effectively characterize CSO impacts and the efficacy of CSO controls.[7]

Those controls are aimed at reducing the occurrence of CSOs and mitigating the after-effects of CSOs that do occur. They reflect a change in the method by which CSSs were intended to be operated and managed that occurred in the late twentieth century, as compared to the previous approaches to CSSs. The most common prior approach to CSSs was to simply enlarge sewers in order to increase the volume of flows that were conveyed to the WWTP. That in and of itself, however, is not a solution.

The benefits of maximizing wet weather flows to the existing treatment plant depend on the ability of the plant to accept and provide

---

7. Combined Sewer Overflows: Guidance for Nine Minimum Conditions, at 1-5, EPA Document No. 832-B-95-003, May 1995.

treatment to increased flows. The consequences of mismanaging extreme flows at the treatment plant include flooding the treatment plant and washing out the biological treatment processes, which can result in reduced treatment capacity and efficiency at the plant for extended periods of time.[8]

The multitude of problems with CSSs, including but not limited to CSOs, were the genesis of the Municipal Separate Stormwater Systems (MS4) which, as the name implies, involve a storm water sewer system that is separate from the sanitary sewers and is created solely to serve storm water conveyancing needs.

> An MS4 is a conveyance or system of conveyances that is: owned by a state, city, town, village or other public entity that discharges to the waters of the US; designed or used to collect or convey stormwater (including storm drains, pipes, ditches, etc.); not a combined sewer; and, not part of a publicly owned treatment works (sewage treatment plant).[9]

This permits wastewater to be treated appropriately and permits storm water to be discharged, in many cases, without treatment. That results in operational cost savings for municipalities. MS4s carry the exact opposite risk of CSSs, though, in that they result in storm water receiving no treatment. Storm water that carries with it oils and other runoff pollutants from roads and parking lots, and carries eroded soils, fertilizer, and other by-products of traveling overland, gets deposited directly into streams and waterways.

> Stormwater runoff is generated when precipitation from rain and snowmelt events flows over land or impervious surfaces and does not percolate into the ground. As the runoff flows over the land

---

8. U.S. Envtl. Protection Agency, Report to Congress on the Impacts and Control of CSOs and SSOs, ch. 8, at 8-6 [hereinafter EPA Report to Congress on CSOs and SSOs].
9. Stormwater Discharges from Municipal Separate Storm Sewer Systems (MS4s), http://cfput.epa.gov/npdes/stormwater/munic.cfm (last visited Mar. 1, 2010).

or impervious surfaces (paved streets, parking lots, and building rooftops), it accumulates debris, chemicals, sediment, or other pollutants that could adversely affect water quality if the runoff is discharged untreated.[10]

Simply by virtue of having storm water run overland for some short distance before entering a sewer of some sort, even storm water that is headed for an MS4 and will thus be segregated from sanitary sewage thus becomes polluted.

> Polluted stormwater runoff is commonly transported through . . . MS4s, from which it is often discharged untreated into local waterbodies. To prevent harmful pollutants from being washed or dumped into an MS4, operators must obtain a NPDES permit and develop a stormwater management program. Phase I, issued in 1990, requires medium and large cities or certain counties with populations of 100,000 or more to obtain NPDES permit coverage for their stormwater discharges. Phase II, issued in 1999, requires regulated small MS4s in urbanized areas, as well as small MS4s outside the urbanized areas that are designated by the permitting authority, to obtain NPDES permit coverage for their stormwater discharges. . . . Each regulated MS4 is required to develop and implement a stormwater management program (SWMP) to reduce the contamination of stormwater runoff and prohibit illicit discharges.[11]

Whether CSSs or MS4s are utilized, any means available that can *reduce the volume of water being treated and/or transported* reduces the demand on the system, reduces the cost of constructing improvements (by reducing the required size), and reduces the cost for operating and maintaining those improvements. While NPDES permits

---

10. U.S. ENVTL. PROTECTION AGENCY, NAT'L POLLUTANT DISCHARGE ELIMINATION SYS., STORMWATER PROGRAM, http://cfpub.epa.gov/npdes/home .cfm?program_id=6 (last visited October 18, 2011).

11. Stormwater Discharges from Municipal Separate Storm Sewer Systems (MS4s), http://cfput.epa.gov/npdes/stormwater/munic.cfm (last visited October 18, 2011).

and the requirement that municipalities have a SWMP are some of the consequences of USEPA interest in storm water demonstrated in the 1990s, the USEPA took its first steps to regulate storm water in 1972. Understanding those regulations and understanding the future of storm water regulations are an integral part of understanding why sustainable storm water and wastewater management is so critical.

> The 1972 amendments to the Federal Water Pollution Control Act (FWPCA, also referred to as the Clean Water Act or CWA) prohibit the discharge of any pollutant to waters of the United States from a point source unless the discharge is authorized by a National Pollutant Discharge Elimination System (NPDES) permit. Efforts to improve water quality under the NPDES program traditionally have focused on reducing pollutants in discharges of industrial process wastewater and from municipal sewage treatment plants. Past efforts to address storm water discharges under the NPDES program have generally been limited to certain industrial categories with effluent limitations for storm water.[12]

This landmark regulation arose out of a new national environmental consciousness that arose in the 1960s. The National Environmental Protection Act, the enabling legislation that created the USEPA, was adopted in 1969. By 1972, the USEPA had determined that two-thirds of all US waterways were unsafe for fishing and swimming, and thus the Clean Water Act was born.[13]

> The Clean Water Act authorizes EPA and states, which are delegated the authority by the EPA, to regulate point sources that discharge pollutants into waters of the United States through the National Permit Discharge Elimination System (NPDES) permit program. So-called "point sources" are generated from a variety of

---

12. Overview of the Storm Water Program, US EPA 833-R-6-008, June 1996, Section 1.1, *available at* http://nepis.epa.gov/Adobe/PDF/20004EUM.pdf.
13. Stephanie D. Matheny, *The Clean Water Act and Stormwater Management*, TENNESSEE CLEAN WATER NETWORK, Sept. 27, 2009, http://lwvknoxville .org/files/TCWN021610.pdf.

municipal and industrial operations, including treated wastewater, process water, cooling water, and stormwater runoff from drainage systems. The NPDES Storm Water Program, in place since 1990, regulates discharges from . . . MS4s, construction activities, industrial activities, and those designated by EPA due to water quality impacts.[14]

Through the NPDES permit process and the development of Best Management Practices, the USEPA has gradually, over the past 40 years, implemented increasingly stringent restrictions on the discharge of storm water based on concerns about these "point source" pollutants.

The National Menu of Best Management Practices for Stormwater Phase II was first released in October 2000. EPA has renamed, reorganized, updated and enhanced the features. . . . Because stormwater runoff is generated from dispersed land surfaces—pavements, yards, driveways, and roofs—efforts to control stormwater pollution must consider individual, household, and public behaviors and activities that can generate pollution from these surfaces. . . . It takes individual behavior change and proper practices to control such pollution. Therefore it is important to make the public sufficiently aware and concerned about the significance of their behavior for stormwater pollution, through information and education, that they change improper behaviors.[15]

The future of storm water regulations is certain: just as wastewater is pervasively regulated, so too shall storm water be regulated at some point. Just as the days of discharging raw sewage into rivers and streams have passed, so too shall the days of discharging "raw rainwater" pass into engineering history books.

14. U.S. ENVTL. PROTECTION AGENCY, NPDES STORM WATER PERMIT PROGRAM, www.epa.gov/region1/npdes/stormwater/ (last visited Mar. 5, 2010).
15. U.S. ENVTL. PROTECTION AGENCY, NATIONAL MENU OF STORMWATER BEST MANAGEMENT PRACTICES, http://cfpub.epa.gov/npdes/stormwater/menuofbmps/index.cfm (last visited Mar. 5, 2010).

But as communities face increasing regulation of storm water, they also benefit from a growing acceptance of storm water as a resource to be utilized, instead of a by-product to be conveyed away and dumped.

> Traditional designs of . . . urban stormwater drainage systems have focused on the rapid removal of runoff water to minimize the risks associated with flooding in urban areas. Essentially, stormwater runoff is treated as a waste product to be disposed of in the most efficient manner, which usually means discharging it into the nearest body of water. Over the past few decades, technologies and practices have been developed to minimize the negative impacts of urban stormwater on receiving bodies, but the philosophy is still one of excess water management, with the ultimate goal of getting rid of runoff water. . . . [M]unicipalities supply potable water, i.e. water that is fit for human ingestion, to their residents. However, many applications such as irrigation, toilet flushing and laundry do not require this level of water quality. These sub-potable applications can make up a high percentage of the total water used by city residents and businesses.[16]

A community that faces lowering levels of potable water in its rivers or aquifers can now view storm water as a legitimate replacement for many subpotable uses. Much of the current focus on these subpotable uses is at the building or parcel level, instead of at the community-wide level. It is far more likely that a building will be constructed with a graywater recycling system or storm water reuse system installed than it is that a community will look at storm water as a resource to be contained and reused.

The water supply for many communities in the western United States is nothing more than glorified storm water recycling. Salt Lake City obtains the vast majority of its potable water supply from Rocky Mountain snowmelt that is trapped and pumped—it is simply storm water recycling on a large scale. The communities that draw their

---

16. NAT'L RESEARCH COUNCIL CANADA, URBAN INFRASTRUCTURE, *Urban Stormwater Runoff-Waste Product or Resource?*, http://www.nrc-cnrc.gc.ca/eng/ibp/irc/ci/volume-13-n3-11.html (last visited Feb. 15, 2010).

potable and irrigation water from the Colorado River are simply draw-ing upon snowmelt and rainwater to meet their hydration needs. Even in those communities, local officials are failing to take a consistent approach to managing water on both sides of the sink (faucet and drain, supply and waste).

> At this time, stormwater management and regulation are divorced from the management and regulation of municipal and industrial wastewater. A true watershed-based approach would incorpo-rate the full range of municipal and industrial sources, including: 1) public streets and highways; 2) municipal stormwater drainage systems; 3) municipal separate and combined wastewater collec-tion, conveyance, and treatment systems; 4) industrial stormwater and process wastewater discharges; 5) private residential and com-mercial property; and, 6) construction sites.[17]

Even the "watershed-based" approach recommended by the National Research Council fails to fully embrace the supply side of the equa-tion and really only focuses on managing storm water discharges (instead of using storm water to supplement other forms of water sup-ply, groundwater or otherwise).

Water supply on this planet is inherently a fixed sum equation. Communities do not, by any method of water treatment, increase the available amount of water. Rather, they convert water from pol-luted water to nonpolluted (or less-polluted) water. The total amount of water available from all sources (aquifers, clouds, water trapped in plants and animals, and so on) remains constant. Communities can choose to take more of the "good" usable water and convert it to polluted wastewater, or they can choose to take potentially polluted wastewater and convert it to "good" usable water (whether potable or subpotable). The primary "large scale" or area-wide solution is con-structing a mechanism to return storm water to some more usable

---

17. NAT'L RESEARCH COUNCIL, COMMITTEE ON REDUCING STORMWATER DIS-CHARGE CONTRIBUTIONS TO WATER POLLUTION, URBAN STORMWATER MANAGEMENT IN THE UNITED STATES, ch. 6, at 391 (2008).

form. The main impediment to using storm water for potable purposes (or for comingling storm water with potable water supply sources) is the contamination within storm water.

There are a number of tools available that can enable nontraditional use and recycling of storm water on a large scale. Storm water contamination comes from a variety of sources. When flowing overland (and off roofs, through sewers, and related surfaces), the storm water can pick up any contamination that it passes through. Current EPA protocols suggest conducting a Storm Water Contamination Assessment (SWCA) in any area where storm water is coming from an industrial or potentially contaminated area, or where there are other concerns regarding potential storm water contamination.[18] The SWCA process involves both analyzing the areas that storm water is passing through to determine likely contaminants and sampling *actual storm water* to test for pollutants.

Whatever pollutants might be within storm water—ranging from simple sediment (dirt) to complex chemical contamination—there are mechanisms for clarifying and purifying the water, permitting its reuse. The simplest means of "cleaning" storm water involves the use of simple, physical filtration.

> In designing bioswales or settling ponds, natural materials can be used to filter out sedimentation and chemical pollutants. For example, bioswales can be utilized that "are filled with an engineered soil medium consisting of a mix of topsoil, coarse sand, and compost to filter stormwater as it infiltrates into the ground . . . the coarse sand maximizes infiltration and mechanical filtering, while the compost provides organic matter to help aid biological and chemical filtering within the soil.[19]

---

18. *Storm Water Management Fact Sheet*, EPA Form 832-F-99-024 (Sept. 1999).
19. Jeremy C. Lin & Dean M. Frieders *The Future of Stormwater Management: Bioswales and Environmentally Friendly Stormwater Control, Part I*, ILL. MUN. LEAGUE REV., Oct. 2008, at 17.

Storm water treatment can range from simple filtration and use of basins and collection areas to promote removal of sediment, to treatment as complex as that which wastewater undergoes.

> In sediment and oil grease traps, storm water runs through a structural device that has a chamber that traps oil, grease and sediment. The solids need to be removed periodically. The advantage of this design is that oil, grease, and sediment are trapped at a location that is easily accessible to maintenance crews. Water entering the chamber could pass over and under a series of baffles. Baffles at the bottom of the chamber could trap sediment, and baffles at the top could trap oil and grease.[20]

Among the various means of storm water treatment that are possible is the use of some form of sedimentation control, a treatment that is uniformly used nationwide as a result of the EPA-mandated NPDES process. As innocuous as sedimentation might seem ("just some dirt in the water"), it is actually a very serious problem. At its most basic level, "sedimentation means loss of soil, which results in loss of agricultural production. Secondary effects are numerous, including adverse effects on water storage and supply, and adverse effects on marine biology."[21] Sedimentation and siltation is one of the most serious water quality problems facing the United States.

> Silt was the second most important source of pollutants to rivers and streams. In an earlier report, *National Water Quality Inventory—1998 Report to Congress* (June 2000), silt had ranked as the top cause of pollution entering the waterways of the United States. In the later

20. Suzanne Malec, City of Chicago Dep't of Env't, *Storm Water Management in the City of Chicago*, http://www.epa.gov/nps/natlstormwater03/21Malec .pdf (last visited Mar. 14, 2010).
21. *Siltation and Secondary Effects of Erosion*, Victoria, Australia Dep't of Primary Industries (last visited Mar. 19, 2010) http://www.dpi.vic.gov.au/dpi/ vro/vrosite.nsf/36ff1eef35fb658dca2567710003f883/c3dab0bc2ae36567ca2 574c8002ccb67/$FILE/EROSION_VICTORIA_appendixsiltation%20(6) .pdf.

report, siltation had dropped to second place. Silt, composed of tiny soil particles, impaired 12% of the assessed rivers and streams, which is 31% of the impaired river and stream miles reported in the 2000 EPA *Inventory*. Silt alters aquatic habitats, suffocates bottom-dwelling organisms and fish eggs, interferes with light transmission to underwater plants, and clogs the gills of fish. The habitat of aquatic insects that live in the spaces between pebbles and rocks is destroyed when these spaces are filled with silt. Loss of aquatic organisms can radically affect the health of certain fish species and other wildlife that eat them. Excessive silt can also interfere with recreational use and drinking-water treatment. The primary sources of silt are agriculture, urban runoff, forestry, logging, and construction.[22]

The EPA's report, *Water Quality Conditions in the United States*, EPA 841-F-00-006, released in 2000, found that 35 percent of all rivers, 45 percent of all lakes, and 44 percent of all estuaries were "polluted" under the EPA's standards. Siltation was the number one pollutant in rivers and streams and the number three pollutant in lakes, ponds, and reservoirs.[23] Those figures have gotten worse in the past few years; according to the 2004 National Water Quality Index, 44 percent of all rivers and streams were reported as impaired, along with 64 percent of all lakes and reservoirs and 30 percent of all estuaries (extrapolating from the areas that were assessed).[24] Sedimentation alone accounts for impairments in at least 15 percent of all impaired waterways.[25]

---

22. *Surface Water: Rivers and Lakes—Water Quality of The Nation's Rivers and Streams*, http://www.libraryindex.com/pages/2585/Surface-Water-Rivers -Lakes-Water-Quality-Nation-s-Riversand-Streams.html (last visited Mar. 19, 2010).

23. U.S. ENVTL. PROTECTION AGENCY, OFFICE OF WATER, WATER QUALITY CONDITIONS IN THE UNITED STATES (June 2000), http://www.epa .gov/305b/98report/98summary.pdf (last visited Mar. 19, 2010).

24. U.S. ENVTL. PROTECTION AGENCY, OFFICE OF WATER, NATIONAL WATER QUALITY INVENTORY: REPORT TO CONGRESS, 2004 REPORTING CYCLE, at ES-2, http://www.epa.gov/owow/305b/2004report/report2004pt1.pdf, EPA 841-R-08-001 (Jan. 2009).

25. *Id.* at 15, figure 2.

That is only accounting for sedimentation *as sedimentation,* and not counting secondary effects of sedimentation (including bacteria transportation, etc.). The primary harm from sedimentation, beyond clogging waterways and eliminating or reducing drainage effectiveness, is the adverse "smothering" effect that siltation has on aquatic organisms.[26]

Effective management of siltation takes many forms. As might sound logical, the most prevalent sources of siltation are areas where soil is open and exposed to passing storm water.

A brief departure into some engineering terminology here would be helpful. Generally speaking, there are two types of storm water discharges that are possible from a site: sheet flow and point source. These two types of discharges can be understood by considering a mountain valley with a stream running down the middle. When rain falls in the valley, it hits the ground and soaks in. When the ground is saturated, rain that falls across the valley and hits the saturated soil all flows gradually downhill, dispersed across the walls of the valley. This is sheet flow drainage—drainage that is proceeding downhill across a large, dispersed area. When that sheet flow reaches the base of the valley, it combines into a stream at the base of the valley and now becomes an obvious, flowing watercourse. This is point source discharge.

With a traditional, relatively flat, vegetated field in mind, most of the storm water flow that occurs is sheet flow. It is low velocity, widely spread drainage. Vegetation in place within the field does a good job of minimizing erosion and sedimentation as the roots of plants hold the soil in place and as the slow-moving sheet flow does not have much power to disturb the soil. When the sheet flow reaches a low spot and converges into a creek or stream, it gathers velocity and the ability to strip and erode topsoil. This is the reason that fast-moving streams have rocky, bare bottoms. The Colorado River in the base of the Grand Canyon is a great example of the erosive power of point

---

26. *Id.* at 29.

source discharges, gradually wearing away at everything they touch (including rock).

While sheet flow drainage might sound more beneficial than point source drainage, two things must be kept in mind. First, developing property necessarily results in the construction of some areas that are "impervious" (i.e., that water cannot permeate), such as the land under buildings, roads, sidewalks, or other solid structures. This means that less land is available for water permeation and that rainfall is thus more concentrated and more likely to have a higher velocity—so the traditional, low-velocity sheet flow drainage is not possible. Second, while higher velocity, point source flows might have high erosive potential, they do not always create siltation problems. The Grand Canyon's erosion has happened over hundreds of thousands of years. The relevant time frame for a municipal planner is considerably shorter. A point source discharge that is contained within an appropriate structure (e.g., concrete or other nonerodible material) can generate substantially *less* sedimentation than even the lowest velocity, soil-borne sheet flow drainage, because the sheet flow drainage necessarily involves *some erosion*, and, as the hard-surfaced discharge for the point source drainage, can get by without generating *any (measureable) erosion*.

When construction generates impermeable areas, it results in more storm water that is *not being absorbed on-site*, and that needs to go somewhere else. If the storm water is simply discharged off-site, it can result in flooding and other issues downstream. The most common way of dealing with the generation of impermeable areas within development is through the construction of retention or detention basins.

Looking at an undeveloped parcel of property, one can calculate the amount and velocity of water that is "discharged" from the property during a given rainstorm. Unless there are preexisting flooding issues, it is safe to assume that the velocity and quantity of water ordinarily discharged before development can likely be maintained after development. When looking at constructing impermeable areas on-site, this will result in a higher quantity of water, potentially moving at a higher velocity, being discharged. To deal with this issue, engineers recommend building a detention basin. These storm water management structures are effectively large storage tanks that can be used to convert high-flow/high-volume conditions into a more stabilized discharge.

For example, assume there is a small parcel of land that, during an average three-hour rainstorm with three inches of rain falling, generates one thousand gallons of storm water discharge moving at a rate of ten gallons per minute (remaining rainfall permeates and soaks into the soil, greatly reducing "discharge" from the site). If a significant portion of the site is paved and no plans are made for the storm water consequences, it might result in three thousand gallons of water being discharged at a rate of 30 gallons per minute (the total amount of water hitting the site remains constant, but because of impermeable area, the amount of water being "discharged" increases). The idea behind storm water detention, then, is to build a basin that can accommodate the additional volume of storm water being generated (i.e., the extra two thousand gallons of storm water) during the rain, and that can thereafter discharge that extra water at the "normal" discharge rate of ten gallons per minute.

To deal with this issue, engineers build storm sewers and other storm water conveyancing mechanisms to collect storm water on-site and to convey it to a large detention basin. That detention basin drains through what is called an "outfall" structure. The engineering plans for the outfall will specify the size of the opening permitted in the outfall (larger openings permit faster discharges and smaller openings permit slower discharges, just as with opening or closing a faucet valve). The engineering plans will specify a size of the basin that is needed to safely accommodate the storm water runoff generated by a specific rainstorm, and will specify the size of the outfall that generates appropriate restriction and keeps the site from discharging water too fast for surrounding areas to handle.

The velocity of the discharge is just as important as the volume of the discharge. Faster-moving water has significantly greater erosive potential than does slowly moving or ponding water—this is easy to observe in everyday life. If one is washing a car and has a particularly sticky bug on the windshield, does that person want to use slow-moving water dripping onto the bug to clean it off, or does that person want to use higher pressure, higher velocity water? Obviously, the higher velocity water is better at removing the bug because it exerts more force upon the bug and has more erosive ability. The same force that causes the water to clean the bug off a windshield is the force that enables storm water to pick up and carry off valuable topsoil from a piece of property.

That engineering lesson aside, one of the primary potential sources of sedimentation is agricultural use of land. This is because agricultural use of land typically involves sheet flow drainage, but that drainage is occurring on large expanses of tilled (i.e., poorly stabilized) soil. For the most part, agricultural siltation is beyond the regulation of local communities. However, there are a number of statewide and nationwide programs (most obviously including the National Resources Conservation Service's Conservation Reserve Program, which provides resources and assistance to farmers in implementing and maintaining environmentally sensitive soil management (and filtration minimizing techniques).[27] Moreover, it should be noted that modern production agriculture includes the use of a wide array of techniques (no-till or minimum till, etc.) that minimize and mitigate soil erosion and sedimentation. No one understands the value of preserving black dirt and topsoil better than farmers.

A second, less obvious source of bare topsoil is prevalent in any areas undergoing development and is squarely within the control of local municipalities (or public agencies that are themselves constructing buildings or other improvements): construction sites. The USEPA maintains the *Nonpoint Source Pollution Construction Site Management Measures Guidance*, which in section III(A) discusses Construction Site Erosion and Sediment Control Management Measures.

27. *See generally* NAT'L RESOURCES CONSERVATION SERV., CONSERVATION RESERVE PROGRAM, http://www.nrcs.usda.gov/programs/crp/ (last visited October 18, 2011).

The goal of this management measure is to reduce the sediment loadings from construction sites in coastal areas that enter surface waterbodies. . . . Runoff from construction sites is by far the largest source of sediment in urban areas under development. Soil erosion removes over 90 percent of sediment by tonnage in urbanizing areas where most construction activities occur. . . . [E]rosion rates from natural areas such as undisturbed forested lands are typically less than one ton/acre/year, while erosion from construction sites ranges from 7.2 to over 1,000 tons/acre/year. Eroded sediment from construction sites creates many problems in coastal areas including adverse impacts on water quality, critical habitats, submerged aquatic vegetation beds, recreational activities and navigation.[28]

When property is being developed, the first step in the mass grading customarily is the removal of topsoil, which is either removed from the site or stockpiled on-site. That leaves both bare earth (without topsoil, and thus unlikely to support growth of plants that will stabilize and protect the soil) and stockpiles of black dirt. The most common means of meeting NPDES requirements for sedimentation control is, unfortunately, through the use of ineffective tools.

Unfortunately, construction site stormwater now is managed all too often using sediment barriers (e.g., silt fences and gravel bags) and sedimentation ponds, none of which are very effective in preventing sediment transport. Much better procedures would involve improved construction site planning and management, backed up by effective erosion controls, preventing soil loss in the first place.[29]

Traditional "silt" control at construction sites involves attempting to stop silt from leaving the site through the use of perimeter silt controls. Unfortunately, there is no single method of silt control/storm water control that can be utilized to eliminate siltation issues on

---

28. http://www.epa.gov/nps/MMGI/Chapter4/ch4-3a.html (last visited Mar. 19, 2010).
29. Nat'l Research Council, Committee on Reducing Stormwater Discharge Contributions to Water Pollution, Urban Stormwater Management in the United States, ch. 6, at 410 (2008).

construction sites. Rather, a comprehensive set of storm water management techniques must be used.

> Erosion controls are used to reduce the amount of sediment that
> is detached during construction and to prevent sediment from
> entering runoff. Erosion control is based on two main concepts:
> (1) disturb the smallest area of land possible for the shortest period
> of time, and (2) stabilize disturbed soils to prevent erosion from
> occurring.[30]

As a component of a comprehensive sediment management/mitigation
program for construction sites, the EPA lists 18 measures that can be
utilized to implement these goals, including:

1. *Schedule projects so clearing and grading are done during the
   time of minimum erosion potential.* In any area, evaluate times
   that are likely to generate a combination of both a substantial
   amount of exposed, unprotected soil and high wind or heavy
   rainfall, to minimize the potential for silt to be susceptible to
   runoff (from water or wind).
2. *Stage construction.* It is not necessary to strip plant cover and
   topsoil from an entire construction site in one fell swoop. A
   community should strive to permit only those areas that are
   actively undergoing construction activities to be stripped and
   left open. Even those areas that are undergoing active construction activities should be stabilized as soon as possible and
   should be surrounded by undisturbed buffer zones. This might
   come as a bit of a surprise to developers who are accustomed
   to conducting mass grading across an entire site (potentially
   hundreds or thousands of acres) and then leaving the site open
   to erosion and sedimentation problems for the period of time
   (sometimes years) that the site remains under construction.

---

30. U.S. Envtl. Protection Agency, *Nonpoint Source Pollution Construction Site
    Management Guidance* (subsection (3), Management Measure Selection),
    supra note 28.

3. *Clear only areas essential for construction.* This suggestion requires two departures from "normal" engineering and site planning. Many communities are accustomed to undertaking efforts to plan sites to preserve wetlands, mature tree stands, or other obvious resources. Undertaking a comprehensive storm water management plan requires looking at sites and evaluating the areas that are most likely to be highly erodible or that have other valuable biodiversity that should be preserved. In addition to "protecting" mature trees by prohibiting construction in their midst, other sensitive or highly erodible areas should be similarly protected by being excluded from construction activities in the engineering and planning phases. In addition, once the construction activities begin, care must be exercised to avoid unnecessarily grading, stripping, or excavating areas that are not absolutely essential to the construction activities. "Protected" areas can be delineated with a snow fence or other clear demarcation. This approach might generate some initial reluctance from developers, but if the areas in question are highly erodible, the developer gains savings from not having to deploy and constantly fix and redeploy costly and ineffective silt management materials, and by reducing the number of acres that must be graded, stripped, and otherwise excavated. Nonetheless, municipalities and public bodies should be aware that they will likely need to take steps to incentivize these practices, either through flexible zoning permissions (e.g., higher net densities within specified areas of a given development in recognition of preserved open space that generates lower "gross" densities across the development as a whole), or through traditional means used to incentivize parkland or other land contributions (e.g., credits against required impact fees, considering preserved areas to be a component of required land/cash parkland contributions, etc.).

4. *Locate potential nonpoint pollutant sources away from steep slopes, waterbodies, and critical areas.* It might seem obvious,

but stockpiles, borrow areas, access roads, etc., should be located away from steep slopes, highly erodible soils, or areas that drain directly to waterbodies. When preparing engineering plans, consultants often focus too much on cost savings during excavation (i.e., minimizing the distance traveled by earth movers by creating multiple borrow/stockpiling sites, etc.), and fail to focus on the environmental consequences of the construction plans. Simply emphasizing this as a priority can generate significant reductions in silt and sediment runoff.

5. *Route construction traffic to avoid existing or newly planted vegetation.* As a component of planning construction sites, construction traffic needs to be managed and directed. In a typical construction environment where drivers are paid by the ton-hauled and have an incentive to increase the number of trips made per day, unless drivers are specifically directed to utilize a given route on a jobsite, they will undertake to find the shortest and quickest route available. This can result in unnecessary traffic over vegetated areas (whether existing or newly planted), which generates additional potential for erosion. Many people are familiar with the process of aerating their lawns after a year's use and walking/playing/running in the lawns, as grasses do not grow or perform well when subjected to soil compaction (soil being compressed as a result of traffic across it). The average adult human will only exert eight to 12 pounds per square inch of pressure (depending on whether the person is standing or running), and that minimal amount of pressure generates enough compaction to be harmful to our yards and to require aeration. The average construction truck driving across a construction site generates 100 to 120 pounds per square inch when stationary (and progressively more compression/compaction when traveling)—and yet we often completely forget to control the paths that will be used by construction traffic going across a construction site. As roads and parking lots will commonly serve construction

sites, those areas that will be heavily compacted and improved can be utilized from the earliest stages of construction to preserve the integrity and fertility of surrounding areas, if such routing is required (and enforced) by the local agency having jurisdiction over the project.

6. *Stock topsoil and reapply to revegetate site.* The first step in many construction projects is stripping and stockpiling the topsoil. This is commonly done to permit developers to get to the clay or other subsoil that can be more carefully engineered and that has greater bearing capacity for buildings and roads to be constructed. After construction, topsoil is sparingly reapplied in some areas that are to be vegetated, and "excess" topsoil is sold to be hauled off and used on other projects. Requiring topsoil to be reapplied in more areas and to be reapplied in greater quantities (i.e., greater depth of topsoil cover) leads to enhanced viability of plants and vegetation, greater potential drainage of the site in the future, enhanced "permeability" of the soil (i.e., the ability to soak up and retain storm water in lieu of discharging storm water offsite), and provides a host of related benefits.

7. *Cover and stabilize topsoil stockpiles.* Construction site topsoil piles are rarely, if ever, covered or otherwise stabilized in some fashion in practice. Rather, topsoil is simply piled in huge mounds that are highly susceptible to erosion. Requiring topsoil mounds to be strategically located, to have lesser "slope" on their sides, and to be stabilized with plantings or other techniques can have significant benefits in mitigating waterborne sedimentation generated from what are effectively huge piles of silt.

8. *Use wind erosion controls.* Communities commonly regulate and require measures to be used to minimize *water-borne erosion and siltation,* but far less frequently address another, equally pervasive form of erosion: wind. Wind barriers can be as complicated as requiring solid board fences to be employed,

or can be as simple as strategically placing snow fences or bales of hay, or requiring recurrent water sprinkling to control dust.

9. *Intercept runoff above disturbed slopes and convey it to a permanent channel or storm drain.* Depending on site topography, there might be some areas that have to be constructed with steep slopes or other conditions that are more highly erodible. To prevent sheet flow drainage in these unstabilized or steep areas from generating unwanted erosion and sedimentation, these areas can be protected with temporary or permanent "hard surface" storm sewers that convert the sheet flow drainage across unstabilized soils into point source drainage through a nonerodible pipe.

10. *On long or steep, disturbed, or man-made slopes, construct benches, terraces, or ditches at regular intervals to intercept runoff.* This is in keeping with the previous suggestion to avoid situations where sheet flow drainage creates unwanted siltation and sedimentation.

11. *Use retaining walls (to decrease steepness of slopes).* Again, any methods that can be used to minimize the number of areas where storm water proceeds unchecked down unstabilized or highly sloped areas (leading to higher water velocities and higher erosive potential) are helpful.

12. *Provide linings for urban runoff conveyance channels.* Some form of surface should be used to prevent point source discharges of storm water from eroding the channel it is being conveyed through. The preferred choice might be to use grass or sod as it reduces drainage velocities and provides filtration and infiltration benefits. If that is not practical, large stones, concrete, or similar materials might be used.

13. *Use check dams.* Check dams, which are small, temporary dams across swales or channels constructed using gravel/straw bales, are another effective means of reducing water velocities and minimizing storm water's erosive potential.

14. *Seed and fertilize.* In flat areas with favorable soils, simply planting the area with grass, alfalfa, or other topcover can effectively manage storm water. In other areas, seeding might be less effective as the seeds will not be protected and will not have adequate root structure to hold them in place during storms, resulting in the seed itself being carried away by storm flows.

15. *Use seeding and mulch/mats.* On moderate to steep surfaces, using a mulch topcover in conjunction with seeding can provide enough temporary protection for seeding plants to establish adequate root structures to resist storm water erosion.

16. *Use mulch/mats.* In areas where seeding is unlikely to be effective, there are a variety of different mulches, netting systems, and other nongrowing topcovers that can be used to protect topsoil. Of note, these systems need to be protected from large storm water flows or they might simply wash away.

17. *Use sodding.* While it can be quite expensive, sod is the fastest way to permanently establish grass with a developed root structure to protect highly erodible areas that are not conducive to seeding.

18. *Use wildflower cover.* Native wildflowers can offer drought and disease resistance, while requiring minimal maintenance and cost to be established. In areas with minimal erosive potential, they can be an effective means of mitigating storm water erosion and sedimentation. However, because wildflowers do not grow as closely together as does grass, they are not as effective as grass in reducing storm water velocities or in protecting topsoil.[31]

An additional benefit of these techniques is that they can result in a more aesthetically pleasing construction site, and, by minimizing the potential for dust storms or flooding of adjoining properties, they can

---

31. *Id.*

reduce the likelihood of complaints from other nearby property owners or residents about construction activities. However, for all of the
benefits of this comprehensive approach to construction site storm
water management, the EPA continues to caution that "traditional"
sediment control mechanisms (including sediment/silt basins, sediment traps, fabric filter fences and straw bale barriers for storm sewer
inlet protection, designated and improved construction entrances, and
vegetated filter strips to protect creeks, streams and rivers) should be
used in conjunction with the alternative techniques described above.[32]

These storm water management techniques are just one side of
the equation, however. They are effective tools for minimizing sedimentation and reducing storm water velocity and related damage, but
even after employing these techniques, there is still storm water that
must be handled in some fashion. The question then becomes what
to do with the remaining storm water. Traditionally, storm water was
funneled off into nearby creeks or streams and sent downriver for the
next town to deal with. A more sustainable perspective views storm
water as a resource to be managed.

Many of the modern tools used to deal with storm water involve
not only managing the flow but also reducing the volume of storm
water being generated. In the simplest of terms, minimizing storm
water volume comes from preventing storm water from running off.
Creating new impervious area generates storm water flow. So the simplest means of *reducing* storm water flow is to reduce impervious area.
There are many tools that can be used. Replacing traditional asphalt
or concrete parking lots with permeable pavement or interlocking
paver bricks stabilized with sand or other similar materials can significantly reduce the runoff generated. Instead of traditional storm
water conveyancing in solid pipes (that efficiently transmit 100 percent of the runoff generated to the discharge point), storm water can
be conveyed through ground-level, landscaped bioswales that permit
storm water to infiltrate the soil and that retain the capacity to con-

---

32. *Id.* at Subsection (5), Sediment Control Practices.

vey excess flows off-site efficiently. Rather than constructing impervious, clay-lined detention "ponds," storm water can be channeled into permeable areas that offer both detention *and* infiltration.

Portland, Oregon, operates a CSS and has invested significantly in the use of bioswales, permeable detention areas, and other forms of storm water technology that reduce storm water inflow into the sewer system. Portland has come to recognize that the cheapest way of handling excess storm water flows is to prevent them from occurring. Areas of the city are being repurposed and redeveloped to minimize runoff and to maximize infiltration. City sidewalks that were once filled with impervious concrete have been replaced with a dual-purpose design. One portion of the concrete sidewalk remains, and next to that sidewalk is a depressed, concrete lined "planter box."

The planter box has no solid bottom; rather, it has soil and mulch forming the bottom of it, with a variety of plants installed in the soil. The planter boxes are designed to have a normal level of soil that is 12 to 18 inches below the top of the planter box, which creates instant storm water detention on site. The planter boxes are designed so that as storm water flows into them from neighboring streets and buildings, that 12 to 18 inches of area is filled with the storm water, which is then stored instead of being discharged. When the planter box fills, excess storm water overflows into the next planter box down the street, and so on. When the last of the planter boxes on the street overflows, the water is then discharged into a storm sewer—albeit at a greatly reduced volume and rate.

The water that remains in the planter box (below the level of the outfall) is left to soak into the permeable soil underlying the planter box. This design (1) permits aesthetically pleasing plants to be maintained (and automatically watered) instead of having less aesthetic concrete; (2) uses space that is already present and converts that space to useable detention area; (3) performs the traditional storm water task of conveying water and preventing localized flooding (albeit while discharging less storm water traveling at a slower speed); and (4) incurs minimal maintenance expense. This technique can be used in nearly any environment and in nearly any right-of-way. Care must be exercised in selecting appropriate plants for different environments—for example, in areas that apply chemical ice-melt to roads, salt-tolerant plants must be selected. In addition, the amount of retention or storage that can be generated is limited by the groundspace available. This use of plant and soil to detain, slow, and filter storm water is commonly referred to as bioretention.

> Bioretention is a soil and plant based storm water management practice used to filter and infiltrate runoff from impervious areas such as streets, parking lots, and rooftops. Bioretention systems are essentially plant-based filters designed to mimic the infiltrative properties of naturally vegetated areas, reducing runoff rates and volumes.[33]

The use of bioswales and bioretention programs promotes significant flexibility in the land planning and design process.

> One design criteria of great significance when retrofitting similar stormwater management techniques and infrastructure into existing areas of a municipality is the design flexibility inherent in bioswale use . . . [B]ioswales and [sustainable stormwater management, or SSM] programs can be incorporated into curbed areas in the right of way without having a significant impact on adjoining property owners. . . . For example, a one foot deep bioswale of 15' x 8' generates one-hundred and twenty cubic feet of stormwater detention volume, without need for a pond or other structure. In effect, a single lost parking space is converted into valuable stormwater detention in an aesthetically pleasing fashion (and unlike traditional detention basins, bioswales permit water infiltration and aquifer recharge, instead of simply storing and discharging water to alternate locations). In lieu of wet or dry bottom grassed detention basins, bioswales can be attractively landscaped planter boxes. [Through the use of bioswales,] [i]t is expected that the water quality of the overall runoff from the area will be enhanced through infiltration of the captured stormwater. A portion of the runoff is

---

33. EPA Report to Congress on CSOs and SSOs, ch. 8, at 8-19.

managed onsite instead of direct conveyance through the sewer system; therefore, the peak runoff events should be reduced by some margin. Runoff will be allowed to infiltrate thereby recharging the groundwater table. The bioswales can also reduce sediment and nutrient runoff. SSM programs carry with them numerous benefits. They conserve land by converting otherwise unused right of way areas for detention purposes and thereby reducing the need for traditional detention basins. They aide the environment by filtering surface water runoff before it enters streams and channels, and by encouraging direct recharging of aquifers with filtered surface water. They are aesthetically pleasing and convert what are commonly flat, turfgrass areas into attractive planter boxes with hearty and colorful plants. And perhaps most importantly, they are a functional means of providing immediate, point source detention of peak flow stormwater which permits greater flexibility in designing downstream stormwater improvements.[34]

Many cities are now undertaking to include SSM projects in their municipal codes, including the City of Chicago, which has adopted an SSM program in recognition of the significant environmental benefits that can be reaped. "In vegetated swale designs, storm water is conveyed through a vegetated swale instead of a storm sewer. Swales increase storm water infiltration potential and storage. Swales also remove pollutants via settling, vegetative filtering, and to some extend infiltration through the soil."[35]

Another equally important means of regulating and mitigating storm water flow is to reduce the amount of impervious area associated with a development project. Between green roofs and permeable parking lot materials, there are very few components of a development

---

34. Jeremy C. Lin & Dean M. Frieders, *The Future of Stormwater Management: Bioswales and Environmentally Friendly Stormwater Control, Part I*, ILL. MUN. LEAGUE REV., Oct. 2008, at 17–18.

35. Suzanne Malec, City of Chicago Dep't of Env't, *Storm Water Management in the City of Chicago*, http://www.epa.gov/nps/natlstormwater03/21Malec .pdf (last visited Mar. 14, 2010).

that cannot be modified in some way to reduce the volume of storm water generated.

One such "green" development tool is the use of permeable concrete and porous pavement—both providing "hard surface" for traffic and parking, while also permitting water infiltration and drainage.

> Porous pavement is an infiltration system in which storm water runoff enters the ground through a permeable layer of pavement or other stabilized permeable surface. . . . The use of porous pavement reduces or eliminates impervious surfaces, thus reducing the volume of storm water runoff and peak discharge volume generated by a site. . . . The success of porous pavement applications depends on design criteria including site conditions, construction methods and installation methods. Typically, porous pavement is most suitable for areas with sufficient soil permeability and low traffic volume. Common applications include parking lots, residential driveways, street parking lanes, recreational trails, golf cart and pedestrian paths, shoulders of airport runways, and emergency vehicle and fire access lanes. This technology is not recommended for areas that generate highly contaminated runoff such as commercial nurseries, auto salvage yards, fueling stations, marinas, outdoor loading and unloading facilities, and vehicle washing facilities, as contaminants could infiltrate into groundwater.[36]

Many communities have been using porous pavement and permeable concrete with substantial success for a period of years.

> In the fall of 2001, [Chicago] reconstructed an asphalt alley using a permeable system. The new alley has eliminated formerly chronic local flooding without using the sewer system and reduced the "heat island" effect by eliminating dark, heat-absorbing surfaces. The City used . . . a porous gravel structure . . . that contains gravel and provides heavy load bearing support, unlimited traffic volume, and indefinite parking duration. In one 40 in. x 40 in. section of the structure, there are 144 rings made of a highly durable plastic, each

---

36. EPA Report to Congress on CSOs and SSOs, ch. 8, at 8-18.

2 inches in diameter and 1 inch high and held together underneath by a geo-fabric layer. The section below is a 10-inch thick, compacted aggregate base course consisting of a 2/3 stone and 1/3 sand mixture. The new system can handle up to 3" of rainfall per hour, allowing rainwater to soak into the ground and thereby reducing polluted run-off and flooding. The system is suitable for traffic, including residential and service vehicles.[37]

In addition to permeable concrete and asphalt, other more common building materials also offer substantial environmental benefits. For example, common "paver bricks" can be constructed in such a fashion as to provide significant permeability.

> Permeable interlocking concrete pavement (PICP) consists of manufactured concrete units that reduce stormwater runoff volume, rate and pollutants. The impervious units are designed with small openings between permeable joints. The openings typically comprise 5–15% of the paver surface area and are filled with highly permeable, small sized aggregates. The joints allow stormwater to enter a crusted stone aggregate bedding layer and base that supports the pavers while providing storage and runoff treatment. PICPs are highly attractive, durable, easily repaired, require low maintenance, and can withstand heavy vehicle loads.[38]

PICP effectiveness (and the effectiveness of permeable concrete or asphalt) is dependent to a certain degree on the soil type and consistency of the ground underlying the hard surface. Even if the surface of a parking lot is permeable, if the ground under that permeable surface has been constructed of compacted clay, the permeability advantages will be lost. However, these technologies show great promise in

---

37. Malec, *supra* note 35.
38. U.S. ENVTL. PROTECTION AGENCY, NAT'L POLLUTANT DISCHARGE ELIMINATION SYS., MENU OF BMPS: PERMEABLE INTERLOCKING CONCRETE PAVEMENT, http://cfpub.epa.gov/npdes/stormwater/menuofbmps/index.cfm?action =browse&Rbutton=detail&bmp=136&minmeasure=5 (last visited Mar. 19, 2010).

handling areas that have significant traffic. The downside to the permeable concrete and asphalt is that to retain their porousness, they have to be maintained using special techniques For example, a permeable asphalt parking lot cannot be seal-coated, regardless of how weathered the asphalt becomes. Also, once the asphalt or concrete becomes worn, a new layer cannot be installed over it. Rather, the underlying material must be ripped out, and a completely new hard surface has to be created.

PICPs are somewhat simpler in concept. The paver blocks themselves are not permeable, but the gaps between the blocks (filled with sand or small aggregate) provide the permeability, as does the gravel bed underling the paver blocks. However, even PICPs have additional maintenance requirements, as weeds and grass can grow into the spaces between the PICPs and the paver blocks can shift and heave in cold weather. In addition, PICP streets do not hold up as well to steel-bladed snowplows as do traditional asphalt or concrete streets. And while PICP areas might not require repaving or seal-coating, the aggregate between the bricks should be removed (usually by vacuum truck) and replaced on a regular basis (every three to five years).

In infrequently used, low-traffic areas, other options might be available that offer even greater retention/infiltration potential, while still providing a semihard surface for limited use. Areas that fall within this category might include gated emergency vehicle access paths to subdivisions, public works access driveways for wells and lift stations, and other similar pathways—in short, areas that the general public does not drive on and that carry traffic only infrequently.

One such option is the High Density Plastic Grid (HDPG). HDPG consists of a series of interlocking plastic panels that are laid out over a semi-improved (compacted gravel) surface. The panels consist of honeycombed material with thin plastic walls that create regular openings; these openings are filled with dirt and then seeded with grass. HPDG "is a flat grid made of high density plastic that is used to reduce soil compaction and maintain infiltration in lawns subject to vehicle traffic. This permits traffic to cross the area and still allow water to infiltrate into the grass."[39] The dirt and grass permits excellent drainage and infiltration, much akin to open, unimproved areas. However, when unprotected grass is subjected to heavy loads (e.g., fire trucks, public works trucks, or even cars), the surface soil becomes compacted and the grass can suffer ill consequences or can even die out and become patchy. The plastic grid in the HDPG system serves to transfer weight from the vehicles passing over it down to the gravel below, and the honeycomb shape permits the dirt and grass within to avoid compaction. However, the load-bearing structure utilized here is the high-density plastic which is quite durable but cannot support very heavy loads. Loaded semitrucks or even full fire trucks can irreparably damage these systems, which means that they have very limited applications.

A second technology with similar theory is the concrete grid pavement system, which uses concrete units with cells containing topsoil and grass. In other words, instead of high-density plastic, the concrete grid forms the load-bearing structure. "These paving units can infiltrate water, but at rates lower than PICP . . . [they] are generally not designed with open-graded, crushed stone base for water storage. Moreover, grids are for intermittently trafficked areas such as overflow parking areas and emergency fire lanes."[40] However, because of their use of concrete, they are much more durable than HDPG, and because the concrete is gridded, this technology can be more cost-effective than PICP.

The most effective means of controlling and mitigating storm water runoff from impervious surfaces is also the simplest: reduce the

---

39. U.S. Envtl. Protection Agency, *Stormwater Management Techniques: Low Impact Development Strategies.* http://www.epa.gov/oaintrnt/stormwater/hq_ stormwater_techniques.htm (last visited October 18, 2011).

40. U.S. ENVTL. PROTECTION AGENCY, NAT'L POLLUTANT DISCHARGE ELIMINATION SYS., MENU OF BMPS: PERMEABLE INTERLOCKING CONCRETE PAVEMENT, http://cfpub.epa.gov/npdes/stormwater/menuofbmps/index.cfm?action =browse&Rbutton=detail&bmp=136&minmeasure=5 (last visited Mar. 19, 2010).

amount of impervious surfaces. Replacing metal or urethane roof-
ing with green roofs can substantially decrease the amount of storm
water runoff generated by building developments. Simply reducing
the back-to-back width of paved or concrete roads can cause dramatic reductions in the total amount of impervious area generated
by new development. Not only do narrower streets cost less to build
and maintain (and potentially generate lower traffic speeds and safer
environments), but they also result in more space being available for
grass, parkway trees, and other improvements that result in greater
infiltration and drainage.

There is still some on-site storm water flow that must be handled in
some fashion. Traditional engineering practice would be to grade parking lots and improved areas to slope toward storm sewer inlets, conveying water directly from the parking lot into the storm sewer. Even in
areas where bioswales and subgrade planter boxes cannot be used, other
technologies are available to provide some degree of on-site storm water
filtration. For example, storm water can be conveyed from parking lots
into vegetated filter strips consisting of grasses and other similar plants
that storm water passes through en route to a storm sewer.

> Vegetated filter strips . . . are vegetated surfaces that are designed
> to treat sheet flow from adjacent surfaces. Filter strips function by
> slowing runoff velocities and filtering out sediment and other pol-
> lutants, and by providing some infiltration into underlying soils.
> Filter strips were originally used as an agricultural treatment prac-
> tice, and have more recently evolved into an urban practice. With
> proper design and maintenance, filter strips can provide relatively
> high pollutant removal.[41]

Simply taking the extra step of running storm water through a small
patch of grass before dumping it into a storm sewer can result in sig-

---

41. U.S. ENVTL. PROTECTION AGENCY, NAT'L POLLUTANT DISCHARGE ELIMI-
    NATION SYS., MENU OF BMPS: VEGETATED FILTER STRIP, http://cfpub
    .epa.gov/npdes/stormwater/menuofbmps/index.cfm?action=factsheet_
    results&view=specific&bmp=76 (last visited Mar. 19, 2010).

nificant benefits both in terms of reducing storm water volume and velocity.

And what becomes of the storm water that is still generated and must be handled? Traditional methods of dealing with this storm water would include conveying it to streams or rivers while attempting to control the volume and speed of discharge (as discussed above). In some areas, storm water is retained on-site and used for irrigation or to provide a source of water (pond) for fire protection. (In rural areas, a large, wet-bottom detention pond that feeds an emergency fire protection pump can be a far more cost-effective solution than providing an on-site well that has adequate capacity to provide fire protection for a large facility.) Beyond all of those potential options, a new concept has emerged: the use of storm water drainage wells.

> Class V storm water drainage wells manage surface water runoff (rainwater or snow melt) by placing it below the ground surface. They are typically shallow disposal systems designed to infiltrate storm water runoff below the ground surface. Storm water drainage wells may have a variety of designs and may be referred to by other names including dry wells, bored wells, and infiltration galleries. The names may be misleading so it is important to note that a Class V well by definition is any bored, drilled, or driven shaft, or dug hole that is deeper than its widest surface dimension, or an improved sinkhole, or a subsurface fluid distribution system (an infiltration system with piping to enhance infiltration capacities).[42]

Under this wide definition, nearly any storm water facility that is deeper than it is wide, and which is intended to drain water subsurface instead of discharging the water to another source (stream, creek, etc.), can be a regulated drainage well.

> In 1999, EPA completed a study of Class V injection wells to develop background information for use by the Agency to evaluate

---

42. U.S. ENVTL. PROTECTION AGENCY, WATER: CLASS V WELLS, http://water. epa.gov/type/groundwater/uic/class5/types_stormwater.cfm (last visited October 18, 2011).

the risks to underground sources of drinking water (USDWs) posed by Class V wells. . . . The Safe Water Drinking Act requires that EPA protect USDWs from injection activities, and EPA has set minimum standards to address the threats posed by all injection wells, including storm water drainage wells. Storm water injection is a concern because storm water may contain sediment, nutrients, metals, salts, microorganisms, fertilizers, pesticides, petroleum, and other organic compounds that could harm USDWs.[43]

Safe and appropriate implementation of storm water injection wells requires a number of factors and BMPs to be considered.

1. Siting: "Proper siting can minimize the impact of contaminants reaching a storm water injection well. As a general guideline, the greater the distance between a storm water injection well and ground water, the less threat of contamination." BMPs include maintaining minimum setbacks from surface waters, drinking water wells, and the ground water table. In addition, storm water injection wells should not be constructed in areas with other environmental concerns (e.g., brownfields, contaminated sites, or sites with significant land instability that can generate sedimentation concerns).[44]

2. Design: "Storm water injection well design features can minimize the risk of contaminating drinking water sources and are often less expensive to install during construction than to retrofit later." BMPs related to design of the injection wells include a significant focus on sediment removal. "Sediment carried in storm water runoff will enter a storm water injection well unless the well includes devices for removing it. Sediment poses three problems: 1) it can clog the infiltration system causing it to fail; 2) contaminants including metals, pesticides and phosphorous, can attach to sediments and be carried

---

43. Id.
44. U.S. Envtl. Protection Agency, Storm Water Injection Well Best Management Practices (BMPs).

into ground water systems, leading to possible contamination; and, 3) wells that directly inject into underground sources of drinking water (USDWs) may have sediment levels that, for hours or days, render the water unfit for human consumption in nearby wells."[45] Common techniques for sediment removal include stabilization of the surrounding areas with vegetation, use of oil/grit separators, settling basins/detention basins, filter strips, and swales.

3. Operation: Operational BMPs focus on segregating potential sources of contamination and preventing contaminated storm water from being able to infiltrate into the injection well. For example, a vehicle fueling station at a facility using a storm water injection well could be covered with a roof and could use a self-contained storm water detention/drainage system instead of permitting potentially contaminated rainwater that flows through the refueling station to be discharged into the injection well.

4. Maintenance: "Maintenance of the storm water injection well is critical to the effectiveness of the system. Routine, thorough evaluations should include: inspection for accumulated debris, rodents, or other obstacles to flow at inlets and outlets; system checks for roots, mineral deposits, trash or silt build-up; ground surface inspections for signs of subsurface drainage leaks; area inspections for evidence of erosion, which can impede structural and hydraulic performance; and inspections of upstream drainage systems for backups or ponding of surface water that could indicate reduced injectate flows."[46]

Storm water injection wells serve a number of purposes. First, they provide an effective means of "disposing" of storm water without adding to the level of creeks, streams, and rivers. This helps to control

---

45. *Id.*
46. *Id.*

downstream flooding and related storm water concerns. Second, and perhaps more important, storm water injection wells provide a direct means of introducing storm water into the ground, to contribute to recharging underground aquifers. With the development that generates storm water runoff comes homes or businesses that use potable water on a daily basis. Storm water injection wells represent an eloquent solution that uses a by-product of the construction of impermeable areas to offset the water use that necessarily occurs.

There are many reasons to implement sustainable storm water planning using some of the above-described technologies, ranging from aesthetics, to cost savings, to the many environmental benefits. There is also an additional, infrequently considered reason: future-proofing. The USEPA has, for the past four decades, marched further and further into regulation of all forms of water. Drinking water and wastewater are pervasively regulated. Storm water is regulated through the NPDES program, and many believe that it is only a matter of time before suggested BMPs become mandatory regulations. For example, the EPA "has announced that it will propose and take final action . . . on a first-time national rule that would restrict stormwater discharges from newly developed and redeveloped sites. . . . According to EPA, the Agency is gearing up to revise the National Pollutant Discharge Elimination System (NPDES) regulations to respond to a 2008 National Research Council (NRC) report that calls for 'radical changes' to EPA's stormwater control program."[47] Much like communities that installed wastewater systems to accommodate the regulations first imposed decades ago and now find themselves undergoing costly modification and reconstruction to meet current discharge restrictions, municipalities and public bodies are likely to next be

---

47. Associated General Contractors of America, *EPA Announces Plans to Regulate Post-Construction Stormwater Runoff, Requests Comment on Draft Industry Survey to Inform Rulemaking*, ENVTL. OBSERVER, Nov. 5, 2009, http://newsletters.agc.org/environment/2009/11/05/epa-announces-plans-to-regulate-post-construction-stormwater-runoff-requests-comment-on-draft-industry-survey-to-inform-rulemaking/ (last visited Mar. 5, 2010).

affected by burdensome storm water environmental regulations. Planning ahead by implementing some of these tools to help control storm water discharges now will undoubtedly save on future costs.

Storm water is only one part of the municipal water equation, however. Whether a CSS or MS4 system is utilized, every gallon of wastewater that enters the WWTP and has to be processed incurs expense for the responsible municipality. Thus, any effort that can be undertaken to reduce the volume of wastewater being treated can result in substantial savings. Some of those methods are directly applicable to the public wastewater system itself.

When water other than wastewater enters the wastewater sewers (and ultimately the WWTP), the outside water that enters the system is commonly referred to as inflow and infiltration (I&I). I&I is frequently the result of leaks or cracks in sanitary sewers, which permit groundwater to infiltrate into the sewers. On the reverse side of the equation, if there is a crack or entrance that permits groundwater into the sewer, then there is also a means for untreated, raw sewage to escape out of the sewer and into the ground.

> The term infiltration is used by wastewater professionals to describe the excess water that sometimes seeps, trickles or flows into old or damaged collection systems from the surrounding soil. Additional unwanted water can also enter collection systems from aboveground sources. During storms or snow thaws, for example, large volumes of water may flow through leaky manhole covers or combined stormwater/wastewater connections. In addition, private residences may have roof, cellar, yard, area, or foundation drains inappropriately connected into sanitary sewers. Any extra water flowing into wastewater collection systems from aboveground sources, either intentionally or unintentionally, is referred to as inflow.[48]

---

48. *Infiltration and Inflow Can Be Costly for Communities*, 10 PIPELINE 1–2, SPRING 1999, *available at* http://www.nesc.wvu.edu/pdf/WW/publications/pipeline/PL_SP99.pdf (last visited Mar. 19, 2010).

For cities operating recently constructed, modern sewers, I&I can nearly be eliminated. But for older cities operating more dated waste-water systems, I&I can represent a majority of all "wastewater" treated through their WWTP.

> The structural integrity of many sewer system components dete-riorates with use and age. This gradual breakdown allows more groundwater and stormwater to infiltrate into the sewer system. This increases the hydraulic load and, in turn, reduces the sys-tem's ability to convey all flows to the treatment plant. During wet weather events, excessive infiltration can cause or contribute to CSOs and SSOs. Sewer rehabilitation/replacement restores and maintains the structural integrity of the sewer system, in part by reducing or mitigating the effects of infiltration.[49]

Other sources of I&I can include illegal connections to sewer systems (e.g., homeowners that tie sump pumps into sanitary sewers). I&I can be identified through the application of numerous different tests. Munici-palities can do dye testing, where certain discharges into a sewer are colored with a unique dye and are then traced as they flow through the municipal system. Smoke testing can be employed where sewers are filled with a thick smoke and crews then observe above-ground areas looking for any obvious signs of that smoke escaping (e.g., broken sewers, down-spouts that have been illegally connected into sewers, etc.). Municipal water pumping records can be compared to sewage records to determine if more water is being treated at the wastewater plant than is being gen-erated from the city's potable water system (although some potable water use has to be discounted based on uses that *do not discharge into the sewers*, such as irrigation or car washing). Moreover, in larger diameter systems, municipalities can visually inspect for any defects, flaws, or ille-gal connections that contribute to I&I, and in smaller diameter sewers, robotic cameras can be used to televise the sewers for that same purpose.

Once problem areas are identified, there are a number of tech-niques available for addressing significant I&I issues. Where damaged

---

49. EPA Report to Congress on CSOs and SSOs, ch. 8, at 8-9.

sewer lines can be readily reached (or need to be upsized to accommodate new flows), removal and replacement of damaged pipe is an obvious solution. In areas where there are a large number of potential underground conflicts (water lines, utility lines, fiber optic cables, etc.) that make accessing sanitary sewers difficult, there are now means available to either install a liner within an existing sanitary sewer or to complete an underground excavation process whereby old sewer pipe is demolished in place and is replaced with new sewer pipe. For smaller sewers, grout and epoxy injections can be used to effectively seal cracks and imperfections in aging sewers. For larger sewers (over 36 inches in diameter), the application of "shotcrete" (a mix of cement, sand, and water) as a liner inside the sewer pipes can also be attempted.

The value of minimizing I&I cannot be overstated. Several years ago, the Montgomery Water Works and Sanitary Sewer Board of Montgomery, Alabama, evaluated 2.2 million linear feet of sewer lines and laterals, and identified 3,394 defects. They undertook repairs to 97 percent of those defects (using the techniques described above). This repair program reduced I/I by 42 percent, reducing treatment volume by over 36 million gallons per year—thus generating significant cost savings for the municipality.[50]

One common problem with sizing a WWTP is accommodating the difference between peak flows and average flows. A treatment plant sized to handle the peak conceivable design flows that could be generated by a certain number of users might be significantly oversized (and thus significantly more expensive) compared to a plant sized to handle the average flows. On the other hand, a plant sized to handle the average flows might be overwhelmed by storm events and peak flows—resulting in CSOs or SSO.

Relative to storm water, civil engineers commonly design storm water systems including detention ponds and basins that provide temporary storage of storm water, permitting it to be discharged into receiving creeks and streams at an acceptable rate (and preventing

---

50. *Id.* at p. 8-10.

downstream flooding). That same concept is now being applied to wastewater. No—there are not many open "sewage detention basins" being constructed in the United States. However, other aspects of the sewage conveyancing system are being reevaluated and redesigned in an effort to permit municipalities to use smaller, more efficient WWTPs while still accommodating peak wastewater flows.

One such new wastewater conveyancing design tool is the use of inline wastewater storage sewers that are bypassed during dry weather but that are used during peak flows to provide additional storage within the conveyancing system. For example, Philadelphia, Pennsylvania, installed three inflatable dams in large-diameter storm sewers, allowing the sewers to be partially blocked so that they fill, using all available storage capacity. This generated 16.3 million gallons of sewage storage during peak demand, which is estimated to reduce CSOs by 650 million gallons per year.[51]

Additionally, some communities are moving toward having on-site, short-term sewage storage at their WWTP, such as flow equalization basins (FEBs). These permit storage of excess flows of sewage on-site, at the treatment plant. Oakland, Maine, installed such a FEB system that permits on-site storage of two hundred thousand gallons, greatly reducing the frequency of CSOs.[52] The concept is simple and is the same basic concept as that discussed relative to storm water detention above. Peak wastewater/sewage flows are contained either within oversized sewers or basins at a WWTP, and the volume and speed of sewage introduced into the WWTP is maintained at a controlled level. The entire wastewater sewer system can be viewed as a component of the treatment process and available "storage" area, and, when combined with sewage flow restriction built into the sewers, the likelihood of overflows is greatly diminished.

Wastewater that is successfully conveyed to the WWTP must undergo treatment of some sort. Traditionally, treatment involved

---

51. EPA Report to Congress on CSOs and SSOs, ch. 8, at 8-13.
52. EPA Report to Congress on CSOs and SSOs, ch. 8, at 8-14.

some biologic process plus the application of disinfectants (frequently chlorine or use of ultraviolet light), and then discharge into a waterway of some sort. Newer technologies are changing the way WWTPs operate.

> The technologies most commonly used for performing secondary treatment of municipal wastewater rely on microorganisms suspended in the wastewater to treat it. Although these technologies work well in many situations, they have several drawbacks, including the difficulty of growing the right types of microorganisms and the physical requirement of a large site. The use of microfiltration membrane bioreactors (MBRs), a technology that has become increasingly used in the past 10 years, overcomes many of the limitations of conventional systems. These systems have the advantage of combining a suspended growth biological reactor with solids removal via filtration. The membranes can be designed for and operated in small spaces and with high removal efficiency of contaminants such as nitrogen, phosphorus, bacteria, biochemical oxygen demand, and total suspended solids. The membrane filtration system in effect can replace the secondary clarifier and sand filters in a typical activated sludge treatment system. Membrane filtration allows a higher biomass concentration to be maintained, thereby allowing smaller bioreactors to be used.[53]

MBRs carry with them some impressive advantages. Higher flow rates (compared to traditional biological treatment processes) mean that smaller equipment can process larger amounts of wastewater. When operating properly, sludge generation is lessened compared to what occurs with traditional treatment methods. Moreover, the effluents discharged are high quality with low concentrations of bacteria, suspended solids, phosphorous, and other similar substances. In other words, the treated effluent is ready for discharge into surface waterways or for use in irrigation. "The small footprint of membrane

---

53. U.S. Envtl. Protection Agency, _Wastewater Management Fact Sheet: Membrane Bioreactors_ (SEPT. 2007), _available at_ http://www.epa.gov/owm/mtb/etfs_membrane-bioreactors.pdf (last visited Apr. 15, 2010).

bioreactors also makes it possible to design aesthetic exteriors that disguise the true purpose of the facility."[54]

However, for all of their advantages, MBRs do have some disadvantages. Initial construction cost is frequently greater than a "traditional" WWTP, and operating and maintenance (O&M) costs can also be greater. MBRs often have higher energy costs in operation because they use systems to clean the membrane itself to prevent bacterial growth (often using high-volume, low-pressure air-scouring to clean the membrane). Newer designs are changing the way MBR aeration processes work, and there is significant hope that these newer designs will operate more efficiently.[55] Moreover, the higher energy costs might be offset in some areas by reducing land costs. Because of the small size of MBR WWTPs, especially compared to traditional WWTPs, MBR systems can be much more cost-effective in urban areas because of the greatly reduced physical size of the plant.[56]

Even as new as MBR technology is, it is undergoing constant change. For example, one of the significant O&M expenses for an MBR system is the scouring of the membrane itself. Membrane fouling, and the increased maintenance required to avoid membrane fouling (and the corresponding costs associated therewith), might be the primary reason that MBR technology is not more widely adopted.[57] However, MBR hybrid systems are now being built that use aggressive pre-MBR filtration to reduce the amount of sediment and solids that are treated by the MBR, thus reducing the need for membrane

---

54. Brown and Caldwell, *The MBR Revolution*, BC WATER NEWS (Fall 2005), at 7, http://www.bcwaternews.com/NationalWaterNews/recycled-water/MBR .pdf (last visited Apr. 15, 2010).
55. GE Power & Water, Water & Process Technologies, *Membrane Bioreactor (MBR) Design Considerations*, http://www.gewater.com/products/equipment/ mf_uf_mbr/mbr/design_considerations.jsp (last visited Apr. 15, 2010).
56. FRANCESCO FATONE, XENOBIOTICS IN THE URBAN WATER CYCLE 339 (2010).
57. In-Soung Chang, Pierre LeClech, Bruce Jefferson, & Simon Judd, *Membrane Fouling in Membrane Bioreactor for Wastewater Treatment*, 128 J. ENVTL. ENG'G 1018 (2002).

cleaning and maintenance. Though MBRs have the ability to process significant volume on a regular basis, when they are designed to run at peak efficiency/maximum flow for normal use, they then lack the capacity necessary to handle peak flows, storm events, or other unusual occurrences.[58] Accordingly, while the MBR WWTP might be small and aesthetically pleasing, to accommodate peak flows, it might be necessary to couple such a system with some of the sanitary sewage storage systems described above.

In smaller-scale systems operating with reduced wastewater flows, some communities have had success implementing recirculating sand filters as the primary treatment method. Recirculating sand filters can best be envisioned as a large swimming pool full of pea gravel or another similar, fine aggregate. Wastewater is accumulated at the treatment location in large holding/sedimentation tanks where sediment is allowed to break up and be processed with natural bacteria—much the same way that a septic system works.

However, instead of the liquid product of this process being discharged through a septic field, the liquid is pumped into a network of pipes embedded in the top layers of the aggregate in the sand filter tank. As the liquid percolates down through the sand/gravel (1) it draws oxygen into the aggregate to "feed" bacteria in the aggregate and encourage further digestion of the wastewater; (2) sediment and small solids still contained within the wastewater are filtered out of the wastewater; and (3) the wastewater receives a highly effective final treatment through this mechanical filtration process. As the name implies, the wastewater is collected at the bottom of the sand filter tank and can be "recirculated" or repumped through the sand filtration media repeatedly until the desired level of treatment is reached. At that point, the treated wastewater can be disinfected (often through the use of a simple UV light disinfectant station) and discharged as a high-quality wastewater product.

---

58. Brown and Caldwell, *supra* note 54, at 9.

While the aggregate in the filtration tank does have a finite life-span and has to be replaced every five to 15 years (depending on flows and usage), recirculating sand filter WWTPs are small, relatively inexpensive to build and operate, and require minimal supervision while they are in operation. Despite their simple design, they have proven to be highly effective at treating wastewater to very acceptable quality levels for discharge.

The traditional theory of WWTPs has been to treat sewage and then discharge it into a waterway. As the name implies, wastewater is treated as waste that must be disposed of. As with storm water, newer technologies are allowing municipalities to view wastewater as another resource to be managed. For example, instead of discharge into a river (or as a supplement to such discharges), high-quality treated effluent can be used for irrigation and other similar subpotable purposes.

> Spray irrigation systems distribute wastewater evenly on a vegetated plot for final treatment and discharge. Spray irrigation can be useful in areas where conventional onsite wastewater systems are unsuitable due to low soil permeability, shallow water depth table or impermeable layer, or complex site topography. Spray irrigation is not often used for residential onsite systems because of its large areal demands, the need to discontinue spraying during extended periods of cold weather, and the high potential for human contact with the wastewater during spraying. Spray irrigation systems are among the most land-intensive disposal systems. Drifting aerosols from spray heads can be a nuisance and must be monitored for impact on nearby land use and potential human contact. Buffer zones for residential systems must often be as large as, or even larger than, the spray field itself to minimize problems. In a spray irrigation system, pretreatment of the wastewater is normally provided by a septic tank (primary clarifier) and aerobic unit, as well as a sand (media) filter and disinfection unit. Some states do not require the aerobic unit if the filter is used. The pretreated wastewater in spray irrigation systems is applied at low rates to grassy or wooded areas. Vegetation and soil microorganisms metabolize most nutrients and organic compounds in the wastewater during percolation

through the first several inches of soil. The cleaned water is then absorbed by deep-rooted vegetation, or it passes through the soil to the ground water.[59]

Spray irrigation carries with it many benefits. It promotes efficient reuse of water and reduces the need to use potable water for irrigation purposes. Under some circumstances, it can convert things that would be "contaminants" in discharged water (e.g., urea, nitrogen, phosphorus, etc.) into fertilizer in irrigated areas. It can greatly reduce the need for point source wastewater discharge. In addition, while performing all of these great feats, spray irrigation systems can be used to grow food (when applied on agricultural plots) or to create aesthetically pleasing areas (parks, golf courses, open space, etc.).

The potential downsides for spray irrigation systems must also be considered, however. First, because the systems cannot irrigate during freezing conditions or when it is windy or very wet, they must employ large lagoons to store treated effluent during periods when it cannot be discharged. These lagoons can require large areas for storage.

Because the treated effluent is irrigated at relatively low rates, a spray irrigation system must have large areas of open space available for irrigation. Even when significant open space is available, the potential for circumstances where the weather will not permit adequate irrigation must be considered (e.g., where a particularly wet season is encountered and irrigation is minimal). Wet weather is an especially difficult issue for spray irrigation systems to accommodate because it has a double impact upon them. Rainfall can both prevent the WWTP operator from irrigating (which would reduce the volume of stored treated effluent in the lagoon), and because the rainfall also falls upon the lagoon, it _increases_ the volume of water in the lagoon.

Some spray irrigation systems are constructed as a supplement to a traditional discharge system or are built with some facility for

---

59. U.S. ENVTL. PROTECTION AGENCY, ONSITE WASTEWATER TREATMENT SYSTEMS TECHNOLOGY FACT SHEET 12, LAND TREATMENT SYSTEMS, at TFS-72, http://www.adwwa.org/tech_fs_12.pdf (last visited Apr. 15, 2010).

emergency discharges when necessary to preserve the lagoon level. Moreover, in areas that encounter freezing temperatures, the irrigation pipes and sprinkler heads must be drained and cleaned (winterized) to avoid burst pipes. And in any area they are installed, regardless of climate, sprinkler heads do require occasional maintenance and replacement and require greater care to be exercised when mowing/maintaining irrigated areas.

Spray irrigation systems are not necessarily limited to large-scale municipal facilities, however. For example, Pennsylvania has approved the use of Individual Residential Spray Irrigation Systems (IRSIS) as an alternative to traditional on-site septic systems for residential use. "The IRSIS was developed and is designed for sites with certain restrictive soil conditions—particularly sites with soils having shallow bedrock and/or high water tables; sites where other on-lot systems would not be suitable."[60] IRSIS systems do require significantly more land area than a traditional septic field (ten thousand square feet or more can be required to serve a single house), but in some instances where subgrade/soil conditions do not permit the use of septic systems, IRSIS can be the only alternative to a "pump and haul" system where sewage is stored on-site for trucking and disposal off-site.

The impact that spray irrigation systems can have upon municipalities should not be underestimated. Many areas of the United States experience frequent periods of drought, resulting in reduced water availability. One of the most popular means of restricting private water use is to implement a partial or full ban on private irrigation of landscaping and grasses. In drought years, when landscaping and grass requires the most irrigation, homeowners are prevented from irrigating because of the immense draws that private irrigation places on potable water systems. In order to build systems capable of servic-

---

60. Albert R. Jarrett & Raymond Regan, *Individual Residential Spray Irrigation Systems*, Agricultural & Biological Engineering, Penn State College of Agricultural Sciences, at 1, http://www.abe.psu.edu/extension/factsheets/f/f169.pdf (last visited Apr. 15, 2010).

ing private irrigation, municipalities are forced to overbuild their wells and storage infrastructure for a need that is seasonal and infrequent. Homeowners end up with costly utility bills necessary just to keep their plantings alive, and much of the treatment that goes into making the water potable is simply unnecessary for the contemplated use. In short, the system is costly, inefficient, and wasteful of a valuable resource. Spray irrigation of treated effluent can be a far more environmentally sound means of managing wastewater, reducing costs of potable water pumping and distribution, and reducing costs of wastewater treatment and discharge while providing an environmental and aesthetic benefit with irrigated landscaping.

Even without proceeding into wastewater reuse, there are many forms of water recycling. Many communities permit and even encourage the use of "rain barrels" and other similar means of storing rainwater on-site (in small scale) for domestic irrigation uses. In addition, many states permit "graywater" recycling to supplement and reduce potable water use. Graywater is wastewater generated by a property other than sewage. For example, water coming from a toilet is sewage and would be discharged to a sanitary sewer. However, water coming from a sink shower would be "graywater" that could be stored on-site and reused for irrigation, for supplying water to flush toilets, or for other subpotable uses.[61]

---

61. For a relatively expansive look at some of the earliest efforts toward graywater reuse and recycling, see Alison Whitney, Richard Bennett, Carlos Arturo Carvajal & Marsha Prillwitz, *Monitoring Graywater Use: Three Case Studies in California*, California Dep't of Water Resources, City of Santa Barbara, & East Bay Mun. Utils. Dist. (January 1999), *available at* http://www.water.ca.gov/wateruseefficiency/docs/monitoringGW_Use.pdf. Their conclusions were that while first-time efforts at permitting graywater reuse in communities can be problematic, successive efforts can be very successful when a community gains familiarity with the problems that customarily arise in the retrofit process. Many of the challenges that their study identifies are predominantly associated with retrofitting graywater reuse systems into existing residential structures, and are not necessarily applicable to new construction.

Where either treated effluent spray irrigation or graywater recycling are permitted, local regulations must be put into place to satisfactorily safeguard the public. For example, if a municipality agrees to permit its treated effluent to be used for irrigation of private property, any such irrigated properties must be subjected to either an agreement or a restrictive covenant recorded against the property, entitling the municipality to maintain the spray irrigation system, to control the irrigation, and to discharge treated effluent onto the properties at designated times and under controlled conditions. These agreements would be reinforced by municipal ordinances prohibiting tampering with the irrigation system, along with an extensive notice system to keep the public informed of the positives and characteristics of the treated effluent.

The municipality would also need to monitor and maintain the system, which would require devoting staff time. A municipality would have to evaluate the spray irrigation system's operating costs to determine if the savings in lowering potable water system operating expenses offset the spray irrigation maintenance costs, or whether it would be necessary to impose a nominal fee for the irrigation effluent. All of these are matters that could be satisfactorily addressed with local regulation—assuming that state legislation is permissive enough to enable such innovative programs to be used.

If state law is permissive enough *and* a local agency wants to contemplate undertaking a spray irrigation program, it is necessary to develop a mechanism for funding the improvements contemplated to be built. There are myriad grant and loan programs available for wastewater treatment plants, both on a federal and state level, but given that these programs change eligibility characteristics on a regular basis, this book does not go into great detail exploring those options. However, when undertaking a project of this nature, it does make sense to investigate all such available options. Even if cash is available to fund construction, some of the government loan and grant programs offered might include partial loan forgiveness or other unique benefits that make it less costly to *borrow money* than it is to simply pay cash.

One other obvious source of funding for a wastewater irrigation program is the reverse usage charge. Users of the system that receive wastewater irrigation can be charged for the benefits they are receiving. Their potable water use is being reduced, and they are receiving the benefits of the public irrigation system, and this is a benefit that can be charged for (whether the charge is a flat monthly charge or whether it is a variable charge depending on irrigation use). Especially where the treated effluent is being provided for commercial use (e.g., irrigation of golf courses, greenhouses, etc.), there are many rational arguments to be made in favor of charging for irrigation. Even if a loan or other funding mechanism is used for construction, a pledge of user charge revenue from the operation of the system can be an effective means of funding the repayment of the loan and can be a mechanism for limiting the debt obligation to the improvement itself (rather than having the debt become a general obligation of the municipality).

In addition, many states have various special taxing districts that can be formed to fund the cost of constructing and operating public improvements of this nature. For example, in many states, municipalities can form either special service areas (SSAs) or special assessment areas (SAAs) to provide supplemental funding. SSAs and SAAs are highly dependent on state law for their specifics, but generally speaking, these are processes whereby a governmental agency can define a geographic area that is to receive a unique benefit from a public improvement, and can levy a tax (either a flat tax or an ad valorem tax) against the properties within that area, to provide funding for the construction or operation of the improvement. This represents a separate tax in addition to all other taxes and fees assessed by the municipality. Because it can be geographically tailored to specific areas that are receiving benefits, these areas can often be created with the cooperation of landowners, once the owners are educated about the costs and benefits involved.

Moreover, in many states, SSAs and SAAs can be used to provide funding even for the "private construction" of public improvements. If a property developer is building a subdivision and is constructing roads, sidewalks, and sewers in that subdivision that will someday be dedicated for public use, the SSA or SAA can be formed to provide a funding mechanism to aid in that construction process. SSAs or SAAs can be used to provide a means of paying off and retiring debt. This enables a private developer to borrow "public bond" money cheaply and with the tax benefits associated with public bonding projects,[62] and pledge SSA or SAA revenue to retire the debt. This saves the developer money in the funding process (public debt usually being less expensive than comparable private debt because of tax exemption[63]), which can result in either more affordable developments or an expanded offering of development enhancements (e.g., incorporation of spray irrigation systems, etc.).

Before an objection is raised that public funds and taxes should not be used to build developer improvements (one of the common objections to SSAs and SAAs), the economics of the situation must be evaluated. If a municipality works with a developer to provide more affordable financing for public improvements through the use of an SSA or SAA, potential buyers (1) need to understand the financing being utilized and (2) the savings should be passed on to the buyer. For example, if a developer constructs public improvements that have a per-lot cost of $10,000 in a residential subdivision, and the developer recoups that cost by selling a $90,000 house for $100,000 ($90,000

---

62. Without delving too deeply into the world of public bond financing, on a general basis, there are many forms of public bonds that are available that offer income tax benefits to the parties lending the cash at issue. Because the lender enjoys tax benefits, the lender can afford to lend the bonded funds at a lower interest rate compared to private, taxable bonds, which can result in cash savings for municipalities and developers that are working together.

63. In many instances, "public debt" as described here can be nonrecourse debt to the unit of local government, but can convey tax-exempt benefits to the developer/borrower, resulting in lower interest rates and reduced financing costs in building and implementing sustainable technology. Offering use of these governmental financing mechanisms can be a powerful incentive to encourage sustainable development practices.

for the house and $10,000 for the roads, sidewalks, etc.), the buyers know what they are getting into. But if the developer sells the house for $90,000, and the buyers do not realize that they also are taking on $10,000 in SSA or SAA debt until they get their first tax bill, that can obviously result in some hard feelings and difficult issues to resolve. By educating buyers and sharing the cost savings of public borrowing with them, a more efficient project can result. Again—the unique constraints applicable in the state where the project is located must be considered.

While taking this brief deviation into the world of financing, one other topic should be discussed: recapture. Most simply, recapture is the concept of charging property owners for the benefits extended to them. For example, assume the Town of A has three potential future developments at the edge of town, such that the existing corporate limits of A are next to future developments B, C, and D (in that order). Each of those three developments (B, C, and D) is likely to have a hundred new homes. If the owner of D decides to build, she will need to extend water and sewer out to her subdivision. On one hand, D could build a water main and sewer line that is big enough to serve her development alone. If that model is used, when B and C develop, they too will need to build their own sewer lines. This results in a number of parallel lines being constructed, which increases the costs for everyone and which increases the long-term maintenance costs for the Town of A.

On the other hand, D could build sewer and water extensions that would be big enough to service all 300 houses to be built in B, C, and D. This results in one larger, more efficient system. But D should not have the burden of building improvements on her dime to provide service to B and C. This is where recapture comes in. The municipality executes a recapture agreement with D, and through this agreement, when B and C want to develop their property, they have to pay D their pro rata share of the improvements' cost. There are some state-specific rules for the use of recapture, but this is the general concept.

Municipalities have become comfortable with the concept of using recapture for hard construction costs (e.g., a share of a sewer main, based on capacity utilized). There might be ways, however, of expanding the use of recapture to provide funding for other less tangible benefits. For example, if developer D uses an advanced storm water management technique (bioswales, storm water injection wells, etc.) that reduces the volume of storm water discharged from her property, that might result in developers B and C having less potential for flooding and thus having more buildable area. This is a benefit provided to them through D's construction of her improvements that could be subject to recapture. This both incentivizes D to build the improvement and rewards her for the benefit she is extending to other "downstream" developers. This concept has some fairly broad limits, providing that the municipality understands and can quantify the value of the benefit that one developer is conferring onto another.

In addition to funding and building the improvements necessary to handle wastewater, storm water, and the other by-products of development, the improvements necessary to provide services to the development must be considered. Humans, like all animals, require potable water to survive. While humans have evolved their water use from simple drinking and bathing into plant irrigation, car washing, and other subpotable uses (some of which can utilize treated effluent and graywater recycling as described above), a development will not be successful if it does not have potable water.

A majority of the techniques available for efficiently handling potable water systems are aimed at the waste side of the equation (recapturing and filtering "used" water for reuse). There are also many building technologies available that can reduce potable water demand (e.g., low-flow faucets, toilets, and shower heads). On the production side, there is not a great amount of new technology available. We certainly have new and more efficient means of obtaining and delivering potable water (compared to the rope and bucket systems of yore), but ultimately, the end result is the same: we take water from one source (ground aquifers, rivers, lakes, etc.) and convey it to people for use.

There are some simple steps that can be taken to make potable water systems more efficient. Obviously, old water mains and facilities that leak water can be replaced with newer systems that require less maintenance and that are more efficient to operate. Moreover, when designing new potable water pumps and treatment systems, one of the most effective efficiency gains can be had from simply sizing the system properly. Properly sizing a well, treatment, and storage system requires evaluating (1) the available electric service (as pump efficiency and sizing will change depending on the electric service available); (2) the flow rates available from the aquifer; (3) the treatment necessary (e.g., radium removal, desiltation, etc.); (4) the peak and average flows; and (5) the fire flow necessary to service the area.

In many instances, a smaller pump that runs for longer periods of time and is coupled with a slightly larger storage tank can be a more cost-effective solution than a very large, expensive pump that runs infrequently and thus cycles on and off. Depending on electric usage and rates in the area, in some instances it can actually be most cost-effective to design a system with a larger storage tank that minimizes pump usage during the day and refills the tank during the evening, taking advantage of both lower water usage and cheaper electrical rates. In areas that have significant fire flow needs, a municipality might be able to couple a smaller "primary" pump and treatment system with supplemental fire flow booster pumps that can meet short-term demand for water flows (albeit without full treatment of the water pumped during fire emergencies).

In addition to these various supply-side tools, municipalities also have one other very powerful tool to help mitigate excessive water use: regulations. Municipalities can implement water use regulations to reduce low-priority water use and to ensure that secondary water use occurs during off-peak hours. For example, a municipality can pass regulations on the washing of cars (restricting personal car washing to certain days or times) and on the recreational use of water (water parks and swimming pools). Municipalities can restrict and regulate

both the hours and frequency of residential irrigation (or even prohibit such irrigation altogether).

In more urban environments, substantial gains can be had by
increasing the level of security applied to fire hydrants, preventing
their unauthorized use. Since hydrants are capable of generating hundreds or thousands of gallons of water per minute in flow, even a short
period where a hydrant is unnecessarily open can generate substantial, unnecessary water use. Employing modern techniques of keeping
hydrants closed can prevent unauthorized persons from opening and
using them. Many such systems rely on magnets or unique hydrant
keys that are used to open the hydrant, instead of the common five-
sided wrench hydrant cap fixture (which can be easily defeated with
a pipe wrench). If such measures are implemented as a component of
regular hydrant maintenance and replacement, they can carry minimal capital costs and can be very cost-effective.

In addition to looking at regulatory means of reducing water usage
and corresponding demand on municipal utilities, there are natural
means of reducing water usage that can have substantial collateral
benefits. For example, protecting and expanding the use of shade
trees within a community can greatly reduce the demand for irrigation water while simultaneously generating increased property values
and other related positives.

A recent study completed in Austin, Texas, ascribed over $133.6
million in value to that city, based upon the assets that the tree can-
opy brought to the city. Those benefits were counted as improved air
quality, storm water runoff mitigation (through water use and through
soil stabilization), direct energy and water savings as a by-product of
the shade created, and reduced use of chemical weed and pest control.[64] A study completed in Sacramento, California, showed that
appropriately placed trees reduce electrical usage by up to 5.1 percent
on an annual basis and can reduce net carbon emissions from a parcel

---

64. *Tree Preservation Makes Cents*, Dennis Brown, City of Austin Greenbuilder
Program, http://www.brykerwoods.org/Parks/Trees.html (last visited October 18, 2011).

of land by up to 30 percent over 100 years.[65] If resident buy-in is necessary to ensure that property owners participate in tree preservation programs, then the study coming out of Portland, Oregon, showing that the presence of street trees on residential properties increased average home prices by $8,870 and decreased the time that a residential property was on the sale market by up to two days, should be of interest.[66]

The benefits of a tree preservation program are objectively described above; even those economic benefits fail to account for the aesthetic benefit that a tree-filled environment brings. It is no accident that artist representations of developing areas commonly depict mature trees and pleasant, tree-lined streets. Tree preservation and planting programs can provide these rewards, but to be effective, the programs must be comprehensive.

A municipality needs to have predevelopment and pre-annexation tree preservation requirements in place to prevent summary deforestation. Some communities pass regulations and ordinances that prohibit or penalize tree removal after the property comes within municipal jurisdiction. Developers deal with such issues by buying property and, before annexing to a municipality, summarily razing the trees on the property, thus guaranteeing a blank slate that can be developed without regard to existing stands of mature trees. Passing an ordinance that penalizes such pre-annexation tree removal can be an effective tool at preserving those mature stands.

In unincorporated areas with beneficial treed portions that are adjacent to developing communities, the communities in question

---

65. Geoffrey H. Donavan & David Butry, *The Value of Shade: Estimating the Effects of Urban Trees on Summertime Electricity Use*, 41 ENERGY & BUILDINGS 662 (2009). http://ddr.nal.usda.gov/bitstream/10113/31642/1/IND44229126 .pdf.

66. Matthew Preusch, *Study: Street Trees Increase Home Prices in* PORTLAND, THE OREGONIAN, Jan. 14, 2010, *available at* http://www.oregonlive.com/ environment/index.ssf/2010/01/donovan_study.html (last visited Apr. 15, 2010).

can do a "drive-by" tree survey and can document the area with ground level and aerial pictures to illustrate areas that the municipality seeks to preserve. Comprehensive plans for adjoining areas of land can not only include proposed street improvements and land uses, but can also identify conservation areas where mature tree stands are to be maintained and encouraged. Using both the carrot and the stick, municipalities can reward tree preservation for new developments, and can penalize summary tree removal.

Even assuming that trees are to be preserved *in theory* during the development process, construction safeguards must be established that ensure the trees selected for preservation will survive. Simply tagging the trees and prohibiting the contractors from cutting them down is insufficient. According to the International Society of Arboriculture, effective tree preservation programs include the following elements:

1. A formal tree survey that identifies the trees to be preserved.
2. The installation of high-visibility fences (e.g., snow fences) at or beyond the drip line of the trees, to prevent construction traffic from entering into the preservation areas.
3. The design of utilities so as to prevent root damage and instability associated with running underground improvements directly beneath mature trees or their immediate root system.
4. Avoiding unnecessary traffic (and related compaction) in the immediate vicinity of the trees.
5. Prohibiting changes in grade in the immediate areas of the trees, such that their roots are either exposed or smothered under excessive fill.
6. Avoiding dramatic changes in the exposure of the trees to sun and wind.
7. Avoiding dramatic changes in soil moisture.[67]

---

67. INT'L SOC'Y OF ARBORICULTURE, TREES ARE GOOD, TREE CARE INFORMATION, AVOIDING TREE DAMAGE DURING CONSTRUCTION, http://www .treesaregood.com/treecare/avoiding_construction.aspx (last visited Apr. 15, 2010).

These kinds of requirements incur costs for the developer. Moreover, by preserving tree stands, a municipality is reducing the "developable" area of a property and imposing some restrictions on the manner in which development can be plotted and constructed. If a municipality seeks to have an effective tree preservation program that developers and property owners support, these regulations should be coupled with an explanation of the benefits of tree preservation and with tangible incentives that reward compliance.

If preservation of a mature tree stand reduces the buildable area of a given parcel, the property owner can be compensated with increased densities on the remaining area. This allows the community to permit the same net development, albeit with the benefit of the mature trees. Similarly, treed areas can count toward park improvement and donation requirements that the municipality imposes for new developments. If extensive mature trees are preserved on a parcel, it might make sense to reduce or offset the requirements for planting *new* trees and landscaping as a component of the development (thereby offsetting the cost of preserving old trees against the cost of buying and planting new ones).

Once the decision to preserve old growth trees (or other similar high-quality environmental areas such as prairies) is made, the process is not over. As a component of the tree study prepared for the area, invasive species, diseased trees, and other less beneficial trees must be identified, tagged, and removed. Moreover, on an ongoing basis, the municipality must have a system of enforceable regulations for tree pruning and maintenance—and these regulations must be tailored to the area in question. An area preserved as a "forest" or naturalized area will have very different maintenance requirements than a treed area preserved as a mowed open space with trees on it.

Separate and apart from tree preservation are other forms of open space preservation. Even high-quality prairie areas or other areas that have distinction for the presence of some unique or especially meritorious natural characteristics can be preserved by forward-thinking municipalities. A program to protect and preserve such areas is dependent on many of the same characteristics as a program to protect wooded areas. The sites must be identified early, addressed by regulations that have enforceability and significant consequences, and protected throughout (and after) the development process. If a community's comprehensive plan identifies a stand of mature, high-value trees that will be preserved from development, and indicates the penalties applicable to developers if those trees are removed (e.g., substantial reductions in housing densities permitted, etc.), the community can build an effective tool to ensure that the trees will be preserved. Given the many environmental, aesthetic, and social benefits of trees, communities can legitimately justify this sort of regulation to preserve mature trees based on public health, safety, and welfare concerns—the ideas at the core of municipal planning and zoning.

One of the most commonly preserved natural habitats is the wetland area. Wetlands are commonly preserved because of the pervasive regulations imposed by the Army Corps of Engineers, and because of those regulations, phrases such as "wetland delineation study" can bring chills to developers' spines. Wetlands are not just marshy low spots with cattails. Wetlands can also be on the sides of hills, in relatively dry areas, on high ground, and in a myriad of unexpected locations. The identification of property as a wetland is not necessarily dependent on ground moisture, but rather is based on the presence of certain plants and soil types (which are usually good indicators of high soil moisture). Identifying and preserving (or replacing) wetlands is a required component of development under federal laws and requires the expertise of an engineering firm with experience and training in wetland delineation (identification of wetlands). Because of the significant level of regulations specifically applicable to them, this book does not go into great detail regarding wetlands and their preservation.

It is worth noting that wetlands can serve a purpose other than simply being a wildlife habitat. Many communities are now starting to explore the possibility of using natural or artificial wetlands as the final polishing/cleaning stage for WWTP processes. This is not exactly a new concept; back in 1978, engineers noted that "natural marshes and other types of wetlands might be useful in providing tertiary treatment to municipal wastewater."[68]

The basic technology at play is very simple. Relatively refined and reasonably high-quality treated effluent is discharged at the "upstream" side of a wetland and filters through the wetland plants and sediment. This is done instead of a direct discharge to a watercourse and provides extra desedimentation, infiltration/permeation into the soil, and greater filtration of the treated effluent that is "discharged" from the wetland. Other advantages include the aesthetic benefits of wetlands (and expansion of their size), habitat creation and preservation associated with maintaining wetlands, and the potential for increased cost-effectiveness in wastewater treatment that can be a by-product of reduced use of artificial and chemical treatment processes. On the other hand, wetlands provide poor removal of phosphorous and some other common wastewater by-products, they are susceptible to climate variations and natural diseases, and wastewater must still undergo extensive pretreatment to avoid the creation of toxic marshes.[69]

Nearly every aspect of development (or maintenance of developed areas) can be done in a more environmentally sound fashion. The environmentally sensitive building technologies that are available are almost limitless. Narrower roads and even the light fixtures that illuminate those roads can be selected for reduced energy consumption,

68. C. W. Fetter, William E. Sloey, & Frederick L. Spangler, *Use of a Natural Marsh for Wastewater Polishing*, 50 J. WATER POLLUTION CONTROL FED'N 290 (Feb. 1978).

69. Isobel Heathcote, *Artificial Wetlands for Wastewater Treatment*, http://wps .prenhall.com/wps/media/objects/1373/1406592/Regional_Updates/update1 .htm (last visited Apr. 15, 2010).

increased service life, and reduced "light pollution" that is otherwise generated by poorly designed or poorly shaded light fixtures.[70]

Also, with respect to streets and transportation issues, some of the hottest environmental topics are those surrounding the issue of efforts to reduce Vehicle Miles Traveled (VMTs). VMTs, as the name implies, are a measurement of the total number of miles that cars and trucks travel within a given geographic area and a given time period. Reducing VMTs means a corresponding reduction in fuel usage, emissions, and the various and sundry other detriments associated with automobiles and trucks.

From a "legal" perspective, the most important actions that municipalities can take to encourage reductions in VMTs relate to planning and planning regulations. Requiring developers to install sensible, linked bicycle and pedestrian paths that are separated from high-speed vehicle traffic makes it possible for residents to safely supplement car use with bikes and walking. Requiring developments to build a small core of commercial or mixed-use development surrounded by residential development within a reasonable walking distance similarly permits and encourages reduced vehicle use. The "park-once" developments discussed in the previous chapter, where parking is situated so as to encourage shoppers to park once and walk to shopping, instead of repeatedly driving and re-parking, both assists in reducing VMTs and allows denser commercial developments.

In addition, communities can undertake to provide safe areas for bike parking and can take steps to encourage and incentivize carpooling and the use of public transportation and, if the community believes it makes sense to do so, hybrid or alternative fuel vehicles. Reserved parking, reserved traffic lanes, and reduced vehicle registration fees can all be used as incentives. However, any regulations

---

70. The International Dark-Sky Association, www.darksky.org, maintains extensive lists of approved fixtures that are intended to maximize environmental benefits and minimize unintended light pollution. This association has an ongoing testing and certification process utilized to ensure that "approved" lights function as designed.

adopted must be practical and enforceable. For example, labeling parking spaces as "Fuel-Efficient Vehicle Parking Only" or as "Carpool Only," as some communities have done, *does not do enough.*

What constitutes a "fuel-efficient vehicle," and how will that regulatory sign be enforced? Whatever regulations are adopted, they must (1) provide a clear, understandable definition of what types of vehicles do and do not comply with the applicable standard and (2) be capable of being condensed into a format that provides those who use parking spots with reasonable information so that they can determine if they are eligible to use the parking spaces or not. Considering the signs from a legal perspective, they must be based upon a local ordinance that defines what constitutes a "fuel-efficient vehicle" or what constitutes a "carpool" such that a violation of the sign can be proven in court. A posted sign, with nothing more, is worse than meaningless. Such a sign means that resources have been wasted on manufacturing, shipping, and installing a monument that is nothing more than a bow to the fashionable nature of sustainability.

Sustainable development requires more than just good intentions and new signs; it requires a deliberate approach that incorporates comprehensive and enforceable regulations. In short, there are many ways that forward-thinking, environmentally conscious communities can adopt politically, fiscally, and socially responsible practices and techniques to help engineer a sustainable community.

4

Sustainable Nuisances and Preventing "Green Clutter"

A commitment to sustainability requires more than just good intentions; the good intentions must be coupled with intelligent and thoughtful regulations that ensure green neighbors are good neighbors. Several years ago, when sustainable development first started receiving good publicity, some developers and property owners saw it as a shortcut to cost savings. For example, instead of building a detention basin and planting and establishing grass around the basin (and thereafter mowing the basin down to the waterline), a developer could sprinkle some "native seeds" and "naturalize" the area around the detention basin. The resulting six-foot tall weeds were passed off as prairie areas under the false pretense that such areas were environmentally sensitive. Similarly, property owners would simply stop mowing some areas of their properties, claiming that they were restoring prairie (when in fact they were simply trying to save money). Those examples are not used to suggest that saving money and green development are mutually exclusive. When properly planned, sustainable development can be very cost-effective. But it is important to ensure that green concepts are integrated into development thoughtfully, to prevent them from being nuisances.

Landscaping is one of the most common ways that communities first encounter sustainable development concepts. Frequently, it comes about as described above—efforts to save costs that are passed

off as being environmentally sensitive. These efforts can be successful and can in fact save costs when they are implemented responsibly.
When communities work to develop ordinances, codes, and regulations to permit the use of naturalized plantings or prairie restoration
areas, it frequently makes sense to work with a local naturalized planting professional who can offer suggestions on what does and does not
work with the geology and climate of a specific region. From those
discussions, regulations can be prepared.

It might make sense to permit some *de minimis* area of naturalized
planting to be maintained without a permit (a restricted percentage of
open space on a parcel of land), and for some types of land use, such
as agricultural land, it might make sense to exempt naturalized areas
from review or permitting processes. But for nonagricultural land use,
when more than perhaps 5 percent of the open space on a parcel is
being naturalized, permitting and review are advisable. The permitting and review process should cover a number of items including: (a)
plant selection; (b) weed and invasive species control; (c) mowing/
burning requirements and restrictions; (d) setbacks; and (e) remedy for
noncompliance with permits.

In terms of plant selection, this is one area that local professionals can offer advice about. In defining what acceptable flora can be
planted and maintained in naturalized or prairie areas, local ordinances can reference specific publications (both privately authored
books *and* publications that are prepared by statewide departments or
similar public entities that deal with conservation). As a component
of the permitting process, the applicant can be permitted to submit
additional suggested plantings for review by the local municipality;
it is possible that the applicant for a naturalized area planting permit
might have suggested plantings that are not on the official lists but
that are nonetheless acceptable.

Almost by definition, naturalized areas cannot be sodded, and
frequently they cannot be "planted" with growing plants due to
cost constraints. As a result, they are frequently planted from seed.
In order to ensure a successful conversion to a naturalized area, care

must be taken to implement proper erosion controls during the seeding and germination process. In addition, depending on local weather, it might be necessary to water naturalized areas for a brief period of time after planting to ensure that the intended seeds grow and can fill in the naturalized area. The biggest invitation to infiltration of weeds and invasive plant species is the presence of tilled soil that is not yet fully covered by native plantings. Thus, it is essential to ensure that the native plantings grow rapidly at first, so as to fill in and shade the entire naturalized areas and keep invasive species from taking root.

It might also be necessary to include some forms of regular weed and invasive species control as part of the initial plant care regimen. Depending on local conditions, weed control might be manual (i.e., hoeing or pulling weeds and invasive species), or it might require the application of some herbicides or other chemicals. Obviously, to the extent that it is possible to do so, herbicide and chemical use should be minimized (especially if the plantings are in the vicinity of creeks, detention ponds, or other bodies of water, regulations should establish clear setback distances from such water within which chemicals are not permitted to be used). The idea of requiring use of local/native plants is that they should be the most tolerant of local weather. Once the initial planting and growth is complete, there should be minimal follow-up labor (compared to traditional landscaping or mowed areas). For example, once the native plants take hold and are growing vigorously, irrigation should almost never be needed, and weed control will most likely be a once-annual concern rather than an ongoing challenge.

The plants selected for a given area might also have other annual maintenance requirements. For example, many native plants benefit from annual burning or from annual mowing; this can promote more vigorous growth and germination of new seed generated by the plantings. The permit issued for a naturalized area (as a component of the review process) should identify any such requirements for burning, mowing, or other similar annual maintenance. If burning is required, the permit should require coordination with local units of government. The permit may require a property owner to notify the local fire department of the date and time when burning is proposed to be conducted and may impose restrictions prohibiting burning when the wind speed is excessive. The permit may also impose restrictions requiring that the property owner have adequate means of controlling an intentional burn and preventing it from accidentally endangering structures, adjoining properties, or persons.

Preventing harm to adjoining properties should be a significant concern for communities considering the potential to permit naturalized or prairie areas. In almost all circumstances, it makes sense to require setbacks between naturalized areas and adjoining properties. Certainly, adjoining properties sharing a naturalized area that crosses their boundaries can be a mutually beneficial option. But if only one parcel is utilizing natural areas, a community might be well advised to require a "traditional" landscaping or grass buffer between the naturalized areas and the adjoining properties so as to prevent the naturalized plantings from becoming a source of consternation between neighbors (if, for example, the naturalized plantings attempt to spread onto the neighbor's property). Obviously, the more area that is permitted to be naturalized, the greater the potential benefit. If there are unique features of the property that provide a natural division that can function to prevent the unwanted and unintentional spread of naturalized areas (e.g., a creek, driveway, or solid fence separating adjoining parcels), other setbacks might not be necessary. In any event, the permitting process *should consider the characteristics of the specific lot(s) in question*, and make a setback determination on a case-by-case basis.

The permitting process, as outlined above, will cover plant selection, planting, and establishing the native areas, subsequent maintenance requirements, and setback/design of naturalized areas aimed at avoiding negative interaction between property owners. The permit process must also address one other very important item: noncompliance.

Ideally, all property owners seeking to establish naturalized areas (whether for cost savings, environmental benefit, or aesthetic purposes) will seek and obtain a proper local permit and will thereafter adhere to its requirements. However, there might also be those who either fail to obtain permits or who fail to adhere to their requirements. Local units of government must be prepared for these contingencies.

For nearly every challenge or risk that a sustainable project involves, there is likely a solution or suggestion that mitigates the risk. Often, the risks are as described above—risks that a party promoting a sustainable project today will fail to properly maintain it tomorrow. Under many circumstances, those types of risks can be lessened with agreements and requirements that permit the local unit of government to engage in self-help to remedy property maintenance issues and to back-charge the property owner for the expenses incurred. In other circumstances, it might be preferable to have up-front security to collateralize the property owner's obligations, and in order to do this, municipalities should look to the enforcement models that they employ in other areas of governance.

Traditional property code enforcement mechanisms can be a component of the enforcement process. Many states have laws that permit municipalities to issue ordinance violation citations and pursue a court-based remedy for violations of local property codes; these can be applied to naturalized areas as well as traditional landscaping. Some states permit municipalities to resort to "self-help" remedies, where the municipality itself goes in and performs required maintenance at the owner's expense; frequently, the municipality is entitled to place a lien on the property if the owner refuses to pay the expense.

As with other potential nuisances, a municipality could require an applicant seeking to establish a naturalized area to post a cash deposit or bond to ensure that the area will be maintained—ensuring that funding is available for the municipality to maintain the area if the owner fails to do so. This would likely be a deterrent to property owners who are considering establishing a naturalized area, however. Any other mechanisms commonly used to ensure maintenance obligations are adhered to can often be applied to naturalized areas, as well.

Many states permit local units of government to establish special taxing districts, such as special service areas (SSAs). In some states, an SSA can be established as a "backup" or "dormant" taxing district. Provided that the property owner performs its maintenance obligations, no tax is levied under the SSA. However, if the property owner fails to maintain the property and its naturalized areas, the municipality can then "activate" the dormant SSA and begin levying taxes applicable *just to the affected property*, to provide a source of funds to maintain the naturalized areas. Other similarly creative local solutions can be pursued as well. The important thing to keep in mind as a community considers these issues is that the ordinance or regulation creating the permitting process must also create a review process whereby the permit's requirements can be enforced on an ongoing basis to prevent naturalized areas from becoming nuisances. The property owner should be required to acknowledge the terms and conditions of enforcement and to submit a written consent to their application to his or her property as a component of the permit application process.

A similar approach can be taken to many different areas of property maintenance. For example, most communities require that there be storm water detention/retention areas to prevent flooding, and many developers seek to build "wet-bottom" (i.e., continually wet basins where the water level increases or decreases with rain events, but which never fully dry out) detention basins instead of "dry-bottom" (i.e., detention basins that are ordinarily dry, but that fill with water during rain events) for aesthetic reasons as a pond can be a very attractive landscaping feature. But ponds can generate breeding grounds for mosquitoes and other pests. In addition, in many areas of the country, detention ponds can build up significant amounts of algae. Any such concerns can frequently be abated through environmentally responsible means if a community is willing to investigate and require such means.

For example, in the case of mosquito abatement, rather than relying on the application of chemical pesticides or larvicides to ponds, many communities require that ponds be stocked with mosquitofish or other similar species of hardy fish that provide natural insect control. In the case of algae growth, there is increasing evidence that some natural control techniques can be very successful. For example, some communities have found that natural, farm-grown barley straw can be used to control or minimize unwanted algae growth in detention ponds.[1] The list of potential concerns arising out of sustainable (or, for that matter, traditional) development techniques is far too long to be covered in any one publication. However, for every problem that exists, there are sometimes more and sometimes fewer sustainable solutions; the goal of a community should be to identify, utilize, and require the sustainable solutions where practical.

These problems and solutions can be applicable to more than just naturalized areas and detention basins. Many sustainable projects carry a risk of becoming long-term nuisances, or carry the potential to lose any aesthetic benefits that they are initially proposed to have. For example, projects to install windmills, solar panels, or other "green" projects can be managed as high-quality, attractive improvements or can fall into disrepair over time. For municipalities that have not yet thought out their approach to such technologies (or to other new and emerging green technologies), the time to act is now. As a component of the evaluation of any proposed green project, the public body must consider not only the immediate implications of the project, but also the long-term implications for the project, including the potential that the project may fail or be abandoned.

---

1. Carol A. Lembi, *Aquatic Plant Management: Barley Straw for Algae Control*, Purdue Univ. Cooperative Extension Serv. Publ'n APM-1-W, *available at* http://www.btny.purdue.edu/pubs/apm/apm-1-w.pdf (last visited May 7, 2011). *See also* William E. Lynch, Jr., *Algae Control with Barley Straw*, Ohio State Univ. Extension Serv. Publ'n A-12-02, *available at* http://ohioline.osu.edu/a-fact/0012.html (last visited May 7, 2011).

5

From the Ground Up: Sustainable Building Projects

It makes the most sense to start this chapter with a brief discussion of what should be the start of any green building project: the development team and the development goal. Both of these need to be defined from the very start of the project.

The development team is the group of people who will be responsible for turning the concept of a green building into a finished product. The membership of this team will depend on the type of project being undertaken and the construction model being used. If a project is being undertaken that involves both an architect and a construction manager, then both of those professionals should be involved, along with an authorized staff contact for the public body constructing the project, the attorney working on the project for the public body, the maintenance department that will ultimately have to maintain it, the engineers working on the related public improvements (parking, drainage, utilities, etc.), and even perhaps some key elected officials (if they are to have a direct hand in the project). It is essential that the members of the development team have enough authority to carry the project forward and make day-to-day decisions regarding the project.

The development team should be assembled as early in the project as possible and should be advised of the development goal for the project so that all understand. The development goal is the guiding philosophy underpinning the project. Why is a municipality pursuing a green project? Is it intended to produce cost savings? Environmental benefits? Positive public relations? That philosophy and goal will drive all other aspects of the development and must be made clear. It will impact how the contracts are drawn, how the building is constructed, how errors are detected and corrected, and many other aspects of the project.

Assume that the goal of a green building project is to build a structure that is as energy-efficient as possible so as to provide for reduced operational costs. That will drive the specifications for insulation to be used in the building, and might result in a "less green" but more efficient insulation being specified. If, during the construction process, the wrong insulation is used, the response might be to require contractors to remove the incorrect insulation and replace it with the material identified in the construction specifications. On the other hand, if the goal is to minimize construction waste, upon discovering the same error, it might make sense to leave the erroneously used product in place to minimize the amount of waste generated.

By taking action early to define the project's development goals, a public body can avoid some of green building's paradoxes. For example, if the project specifications call for the use of a carpet adhesive that is natural/nontoxic and the flooring contractor erroneously uses a traditional/toxic adhesive, what should the response be? Does it make more sense to use *more toxic solvents* to remove the traditional adhesive and replace it with the natural adhesive, or does that not make sense? The development team can make informed decisions on issues such as this if they understand what the goals and objectives of the local unit of government are.

In a real-life example, one rural community undertaking a LEED building project found that the only way to earn credit for recycling building materials was to spend a significant amount of time and use a significant amount of fuel to truck construction debris several hundred miles. At that point, the community had to decide whether the project's goal of building an environmentally sensitive project was best accomplished by incurring that expense and trucking the materials a significant distance, or whether it was best accomplished by using a local landfill that resulted in no recycling—but also resulted in a 95 percent reduction in trucking expense and waste-hauling fuel use. A community whose goal is to obtain a certain level of LEED certification might decide to haul the waste farther to have it recycled. A community whose goal is to build with the least impact upon the environment might make a different decision.

The point of this discussion is not to suggest that any particular goal—whether it be reducing construction cost, reducing operating expense, obtaining LEED certification, or minimizing environmental impact—is better or worse than another goal. The point is to simply note that unless a party undertaking a green building project clearly defines what its goals are from the outset of the project, then (1) its goals are far less likely to be achieved, and (2) it is far more likely that as the project progresses, there will be conflict between work done on the project and the (unspecified) expectations of the local agency.

Defining the goal gives the development team the information it needs to advance the project. The professionals involved can make better suggestions about managing the project if they understand the ultimate goal. If the goal is LEED certification, then there will be no question that the expense of hiring a LEED commissioning agent is a necessary expense. If, on the other hand, the goal is simply to build in a sustainable fashion, that may or may not be the answer. LEED certification is certainly a noble goal and, while imperfect, does provide a tangible indicia of a project owner's efforts to build in an environmentally friendly manner.

Each member of the development team is responsible for making sure that their particular part of the development-related work satisfies the ultimate development goal. In the particular case of attorneys, their obligation is to ensure that the development contracts, specifications, and related documentation clearly specify the sustainability requirements. If specific, environmentally friendly building materials are required, the specifications must so indicate. If waste recycling or reuse is required, the contracts must so obligate the contractors. Because some of the benefits of green building are somewhat subjective or nebulous (e.g., the noneconomic benefits of green building), it might make sense to include express, liquidated damages provisions explaining what happens if the sustainability requirements are violated or if, for example, inappropriate building materials are used.

In some instances, it might make sense to develop a stand-alone "sustainability guide" that is incorporated as an exhibit into all bid specifications and development contracts. This document provides basic guidance on the sustainability requirements for the project. It might require contractors to obtain preapproval on material selections to ensure that sustainability goals are achieved. It might require recycling or other programs designed to minimize waste generation.

Waste disposal and recycling seem to be a common problem for sustainable building projects. Many developers and communities have undertaken to build a LEED-certified project with the best of intentions for waste disposal, only to find that one or more subcontractors fail to follow the green building requirements. For that reason, if a community is undertaking a green building project, it might make sense to require all contractors and subcontractors to use a common waste disposal contractor. All waste can be taken to a common area, where it is sorted and segregated by the waste disposal contractor. This assures that recycling guidelines can be satisfied and that one specific party will have accountability for waste removal and recycling.

The best start to a sustainable building project comes when the party undertaking the project (1) starts by clearly and expressly defining its sustainability goals for the project and (2) assembles a team of professionals who will be responsible for carrying the project forward and informs this team of the development goal so that it can be implemented and achieved.

One of the most common green building buzz concepts must be discussed: LEED certification. LEED stands for Leadership in Energy and Environmental Design, and is a series of standards on building design, construction, and operation that have been promulgated by the U.S. Green Building Council as a component of their efforts to provide a consistent, relatively objective set of sustainability guidelines by which green building projects can be measured.[1] LEED projects are intended to promote the design and construction of environmentally sensitive, sustainable building projects that achieve the symbiotic goals of protecting the environment *and* minimizing long-term energy use and resulting operating costs for buildings.

If a municipality undertakes a building project for which it wishes to obtain LEED certification, the municipality will need to work with LEED-accredited professionals on project design and on ultimate project evaluation and certification. If LEED accreditation is the goal, then the design of the whole project should focus on achieving that goal. LEED accreditation standards should inform the design and construction of the project.

Those who undertake a project with LEED certification in mind must understand that it is not a one-time, static process. LEED certification involves not only the initial time-of-construction review and approval, but also continuing recertification while the building is in use. Under version 3 of the LEED standards promulgated by the USGBC, LEED-certified building owners are required to submit operational data for their buildings on a recurring basis for a period of at least five years. USGBC also has the power to "decertify" a building if it is not performing. The data disclosure is accomplished through one of the following means: (1) biannual recertification using the

---

1. *What LEED Is.* U.S. Green Building Council (USGBC), http://www.usgbc.org/DisplayPage.aspx?CMSPageID=1988 (last visited May 10, 2011).

LEED for Existing Buildings guide; (2) providing ongoing data to the USGBC regarding utility usage; or (3) granting the USGBC permission to conduct their own investigation of utility usage.[2]

This continuing obligation to maintain ongoing data for certification has unexpected consequences. For example, if a green building falls into foreclosure and there is a resulting failure to maintain certification documentation, the building can unintentionally lose LEED accreditation, thus further reducing the value of the building. This risk should be considered where a municipality is granting some preferential treatment to construction projects based upon LEED certification: even if a building is initially LEED-certified, it might not perform properly and might not be able to maintain its certification.

And even if it does perform, the owners/tenants might fail to properly document that performance or might fail to timely resubmit for ongoing LEED certification. In some instances, concerns have arisen where public entities build and own LEED-certified projects and lease out space within the projects. If tenants fail to take proper actions to ensure that certification can be maintained, the governmental entity that undertakes a LEED-certified building project might unwittingly lose that status.

In terms of defining project goals, a party considering a building project must determine whether the goal is to obtain LEED certification, or whether the goal is to be as environmentally friendly as possible. Those two goals might not always be in sync simply because LEED certification standards are intended to be uniformly applied and might not be responsive to the unique nuances of a specific building project. Moreover, a community might decide—without pursuing LEED certification—to undertake a project that does in fact comply with LEED

---

2. Tamara Boeck, Stoel Rives LLP, *LEED Decertification*, July 24, 2009, http://www.aheadofschedulelaw.com/2009/07/articles/design-professionals-and-claim/leed-decertification/ (last visited Feb. 28, 2010).

requirements simply to spare the cost of initial LEED commissioning and subsequent certification documentation and maintenance.

Some critics of the LEED certification process pick out specific instances where it rewards behavior that is not necessarily environmentally sustainable or responsible. "[T]he wide scope of the program, many in the industry point out . . . means that buildings have been able to get certified by accumulating most of their points through features like bamboo flooring, while paying little attention to optimizing energy use."[3] In unique circumstances, LEED requirements for the recycling of construction waste can operate to require a unit of government to incur a heavy environmental and economic penalty to haul waste significant distances to the closest available recycling facility. Some communities obtain LEED credit for hollow efforts, such as posting "fuel efficient vehicle parking only" signs, without any corresponding standards or enforcement.

Some communities have undertaken sustainability goals that address all development within the community, instead of focusing on a specific building or development. For example, New York City has passed a set of building regulations with the stated goal of reducing carbon emissions by 30 percent by the year 2030. Building operations accounted for 79 percent of the city's greenhouse gas emissions in 2009. This legislation requires owners of large buildings to conduct energy audits and to conduct regular maintenance to keep buildings energy-efficient, and imposes requirements for new construction. While the legislation once imposed a requirement that building owners actively engage in renovations that improve the energy efficiency of buildings (akin to regulations under the Americans with Disabilities Act that require ADA compliance be built into many building

---

3. Mireya Navarro, *Some Buildings Not Living Up to Green Label*, Aug. 3, 2009, http://www.nytimes.com/2009/08/31/science/earth/31leed.html?pagewanted=all (last visited Nov. 8, 2011).

renovations), this requirement was eliminated based on firm resistance from building developers and owners.[4]

Similarly, Rhode Island Senate Bill 0232 requires many public
building and renovation projects to "be designed and constructed to
at least the LEED certified or an equivalent high performance green
building standard," with the Department of Administration responsible for overseeing and implementing regulations to ensure compliance with the law.[5]

On the other hand, in some communities, environmental groups
have *actively opposed* green building legislation.[6] For example, the
Sierra Club and the National Resources Defense Council took action
to oppose proposed green building code legislation in California, saying that it was not "tough enough." The legislation at issue was the
nation's first green building code which required, among other things
(a) 20 percent reduction in water use within new buildings; (b) use of
energy-efficient appliances throughout; (c) recycling of at least half of
all construction waste; and (d) the hold-back of certificates of occupancy for any building until an energy efficiency audit was successfully passed.

The claims of the environmental groups that opposed the regulations were, effectively, that the state of California was engaging in
so-called "greenwashing," by promulgating green building standards
that were not truly sustainable. While it might seem that environmentalists would support such an effort, in reality, many opposed the

4. *City Council Passes Green Building Laws*, Crain's, Dec. 9, 2009, http://www
.crainsnewyork.com/article/20091209/FREE/912099982/1058 (last visited Mar.
1, 2010).
5. R.I. Green Buildings Act, R.I. Gen. Laws ch. 37-24, *available at* http://www.
rilin.state.ri.us/BillText09/SenateText09/S0232B.pdf (last visited Feb. 27, 2010).
6. Margot Roosevelt, *Environmental Groups Try to Block Parts of California's Green
Building Code*, Jan. 11, 2010, *available at* http://articles.latimes.com/2010/jan/11/
business/la-fi-green-building11-2010jan11 (last visited Oct. 13, 2011).

passage of the initiative. This opposition was based, at least in part, upon a concern that the standards were too lax and would create less effective sustainable building projects that would compete with LEED accredited projects.

These, and similar legislative efforts aimed at improving the environmental sensitivity of private development projects, have led to questions as to the scope of governmental authority to require green building practices. For example, in July of 2009, a number of HVAC institutes, distributors, and contractors filed a lawsuit against the city of Albuquerque, alleging that a green building code passed by the city that regulated HVAC systems was preempted by federal regulations promulgated by the Department of Energy.

The basic concern raised by the litigants is simple: if each municipality passes its own green building code, the resulting lack of nationwide uniformity creates an untenable situation. The HVAC plaintiffs were successful in obtaining a preliminary injunction against the city, which precluded the city from enforcing provisions of its green building code. In her opinion supporting that injunction, U.S. District Court for the District of New Mexico Judge Martha Vazquez wrote: "the City's goals [in enacting the disputed code] are laudable. Unfortunately, the drafters of the code were unaware of the long-standing federal statutes governing the energy efficiency of certain HVAC and water heating products and expressly preempting state regulation of these products when the code was drafted and, as a result, the code, as enacted, infringes on an area preempted by federal law."[7]

In response to challenges of that nature, some communities have adopted a more limited approach to green building legislation. One approach is that of the city of Alexandria, Virginia, which has

---

7. Stephen T. Del Percio, *The Green Law Landscape*, ECO STRUCTURE, Apr. 1, 2009, *available at* http://www.eco-structure.com/legal-issues/the-green-law-landscape.aspx (last visited Feb. 28, 2010).

adopted a "Green Building Policy," but not green building regulations. According to the policy "The City will continue to lead by example through its own public buildings, establish a policy for new private buildings and will make efforts to educate the public, especially the building and development community, about the benefits of green buildings. The City will also take a leadership role to mandate sustainable design for all public buildings. The City will not be adopting a new code to mandate its Green Building Policy. That approach is not legally authorized. Nor is it necessarily desirable." The city requires independent, third-party verification of green building status from an approved and accredited source.[8]

Another potential approach is to incentivize green building projects by giving unique permissions, such as tax credits or special building conditions. For example, in Los Angeles and San Francisco, buildings that are proposed to be certified to LEED Silver and LEED Gold, respectively, are eligible for special "fast-tracked" development approval.[9] Baltimore County, Maryland, offers a 60 percent reduction in property taxes for a three-year minimum period for residential structures constructed to a LEED Gold standard.[10] A relatively expansive list of green building regulations being adopted nationwide is provided by the USGBC at their website, http://www.usgbc.org.

---

8. City of Alexandria Green Building Policy (2009), http://alexandria.gov/uploadedFiles/planning/info/GreenBuildingPolicyhandout.pdf (last visited Oct. 13, 2011).

9. Jason W. Armstrong, LEED *Buildings Come With a Cost*, Daily Journal, Jan. 11, 2010, *available at* http://www.msrlegal.com/mediafiles/leed-buildings-come-with-a-cost.pdf (last visited Feb. 28, 2010).

10. Rich Cartlidge, *Maryland: We Do Crabs! We Do Football! We Do Green Homes?*, Dec. 26, 2009, http://72.32.52.107/richcartlidge/9209/maryland-we-do-crabs-we-do-football-we-do-green-homes?ref=node_other_posts_by (last visited Oct. 13, 2011).

Whether a community undertakes sustainable development by building green projects through its own efforts or by requiring (or encouraging) private developers to undertake green projects, there are a number of risks unique to sustainable development. First and foremost, sustainable building projects create distinct new potential errors that might not be addressed by traditional building models.

In designing a traditional building, a project owner would ordinarily require contractors to maintain liability insurance, would require architects and design professionals to have professional liability and errors/omissions coverage, and would require the posting of performance and payment bonds to ensure that the project is completed and funds are properly disbursed. However, none of these traditional forms of security and insurance address issues associated with green building. What if the project is completed and fails to achieve the desired LEED certification? What if the failure to be certified is the result of an error by either a design professional or a contractor?

These problems have developed at a pace that has outstripped the insurance market. There are not many products in the way of insurance that can adequately secure a building owner's expectation that it will be constructed in an environmentally sound fashion or will perform to a desired specification. While malpractice insurance might cover design defects, it very well might not cover environmental sustainability concerns.

At the very least, a municipality undertaking a sustainable project should undertake to review the policies provided so that it can understand what sorts of risks are and are not insured. While there are not many (if any) products of this type on the market today, the future might bring insurance policies or riders directed specifically at these risks. In addition, it might be possible to utilize traditional forms of security in unorthodox ways. A letter of credit or performance bond could, theoretically, be amended to secure the performance of work in compliance with specific requirements, such as the sustainability guidelines described above.

The green market might have turned a corner, however, as Fireman's Fund, Zurich Insurance, and Lexington Insurance (among others) have all offered green-building-related endorsements on builder's risk insurance policies—so for the building owner, it is at least theoretically possible to require contractors to procure green-building-specific coverage.[11]

However, no amount of planning can ensure that a building will obtain LEED certification. Nearly all contracts to retain environmental/LEED consultants include a specific disclaimer that the consultant or contractor will work to achieve a sustainability goal but does not guarantee a specific outcome. "Despite the intentions announced when the building breaks ground, an owner and his or her team do not know whether or not a building passes the LEED qualifications until *after* a structure is built. LEED certification is based upon the number of credits a building racks up in the construction process. Credits are awarded for everything from meeting certain efficiency standards to using sustainable building supplies. But when a building fails to reach the credit total needed for certification, it can have a significant financial impact on the project."[12]

One such example of green building gone bad is *Southern Builders v. Shaw Development*, No. 19-C-07-11405 (Somerset Co. Md. Cir. Ct., filed Feb. 7, 2007). This project involved construction of a roughly $7.5 million residential condominium project on Chesapeake Bay in Crisfield, Maryland. Under applicable state law, if the building achieved a Silver LEED accreditation, the owners of the building would have

---

11. David Scott, *Current Trends in Green Building Insurance*, Ohio Green Building Law Blog (Feb. 26, 2010), http://ohiogreenbuildinglaw.com/2010/02/26/current-trends-in-green-building-insurance/ (last visited Oct. 13, 2011).

12. Kyle Swenson, *When Green Goes Bad*, July 13, 2009, http://www.nashvillepost.com/news/2009/7/13/when_green_goes_bad (last visited Feb. 28, 2010).

been eligible for a substantial tax credit. The building failed to achieve the desired LEED accreditation.

Southern Builders, one of the contractors involved in the project, filed suit in an effort to foreclose on a mechanic's lien for $54,000. The project owner countersued for $1.3 million, of which $635,000 was related to the tax credits that were lost when the building failed to achieve silver LEED status.[13]

Cases of this nature present novel issues that the law has not yet fully addressed. Accordingly, one of the biggest challenges of green building projects is that the parties undertaking the project do not necessarily have certainty as to how disputes will ultimately be resolved. With "traditional" building projects, an impartial observer possessing all relevant facts can apply known legal standards to determine the likely outcome. With green building projects, those kind of predictive efforts are not nearly as reliable.

Another challenge to LEED projects is that many of the potential errors cannot be "undone." If a construction error occurs during the construction of a traditional building, in most instances it can be corrected or the work in question can be redone. But many risks for LEED projects cannot similarly be "fixed." For example, if construction materials are required to be recycled and a contractor errantly disposes of materials, that is not an error that can be corrected. Because of the nature of LEED accreditation, green building can lend itself to situations where subcontractors or those not directly aware of the green building goals can unwittingly threaten the project's success.

> After the planning phase, work on the project begins, and the property owner or architect will depend upon each supplier and subcontractor to perform its work or deliver its materials to qualify for the LEED credit. Work performed or supplies delivered incorrectly can

---

13. Karen Martin, *Legal Implications of Green Building, Part I: The US Litigation and Claims Experience,* http://www.fmc-law.com/upload/en/publications/2010/Margin_Karen_Green_Building_Article.pdf (last visited Nov. 8, 2011).

easily result in the loss of a LEED point. Let's take the example of concrete. The LEED system requires concrete used in the parking lot or a rooftop to be a certain color to achieve LEED credit (LEED credit 7.1 requires concrete to meet certain color requirements to reduce the "heat island effect" for example). Let's say that the concrete subcontractor is a bit asleep at the wheel, and pours the wrong concrete. The concrete solidifies and the owner/architect did not notice until a few days (if not later!) that the concrete is incorrect. That LEED point is lost.[14]

Some of these risks can be addressed by having a uniform sustainability guideline as a project form that is incorporated into all contracts, material specifications, subcontracts, and related documents.

Another uniquely difficult issue with respect to green building projects is simply assessing blame when an issue is discovered. "For example, if an engineer designs an HVAC system and it is installed properly, yet the system fails to achieve the desired [energy efficiency], fault is likely with the design team. However, if on paper the design is flawless, but a problem occurs in the installation, contractors will be targeted."[15]

In the real world, it is often difficult to ascertain if an issue is related to design or installation. To the building owner, it is clear that there is an issue—but the contractor blames the design, and the designer blames the contractor. If a system is installed as designed but still does not perform, does fault go to the designer or to the party responsible for energy modeling? In actual experience with LEED building projects, these "battles of the experts" can arise rapidly with each party involved in the project—from design to installation—pointing the finger of blame at other parties.

---

14. Scott Wolfe Jr., *Uh-Oh: I Made a LEED Mistake and Don't Know What to Do*, Green Building Law Blog (Dec. 29, 2009), http://www.lagreenlaw.com/2009/12/uh-oh-i-made-a-leed-mistake-and-dont-know-what-to-do/ (last visited Mar. 1, 2010).

15. Swenson, *supra* note 12.

In resolving these disputes, as in many construction-related arguments, it is often necessary to bring in disinterested experts (i.e., experts who are not involved in the project). Certainly, the first line of response is to rely on the development team and the expertise amassed there. But in a true dispute, everyone involved should recognize that the construction manager, architect, and other similar members of the development team are working for the owner of the project and ultimately (frequently) serve as advocates for the owner. Assuming that expertise has been amassed and the problems have been identified, there are still a series of hurdles, unique to green building, that the owner must overcome.

> One question that has arisen in LEED construction projects is whose responsibility is it to see that the project meets LEED standards. . . . [M]any construction projects . . . use standard forms (usually the AIA forms), which state only that the contractor must build according to designs and standards. Assuming the contract provides nothing further, the question becomes: is the contractor liable if the project is not LEED-certified? . . . Or what if the contract states only that the project is designed to comply with the LEED standards but does not discuss responsibility for building accordingly?[16]

This is the basic question of contract law: did the contract obligate the contractors to do something that they failed to do (or vice versa). The contract *must be specific enough that if a nonsustainable error is made, that error breaches the terms of the contract.* This might be yet another reason for the sustainable building addendum discussed at the beginning of this chapter. Using the floor installation example, if the contractor uses a traditional adhesive instead of the (requested) organic/low VOC/otherwise green adhesive, can the owner point to

---

16. Jacob A. Manning, *LEED Could Lead to Litigation,* Aug. 14, 2009, http://www
   .martindale.com/construction-law/article_Dinsmore-Stohl-LLP_776360.htm
   (last visited Feb. 28, 2010).

a specific provision in the contract that has been violated? Was the adhesive specification incorporated into the flooring contractor's contract? This example is also yet another reason to consider requiring preapproval from either the architect or construction manager for use of any building materials on-site.

In the *Southern Builders* case discussed above, the contract specifications indicated that the project was "intended to comply with a Silver Certification Level according to the USGBC's LEED Rating System." That relatively limited language almost certainly does not go far enough to be of much use in construction-related litigation. Clearly defining expectations and requirements not only prevents problems from occurring, but it also aids in the resolution of conflicts that do arise.

There are a number of approaches to the quandary of what form of contract should be used for a sustainable building project. Some owners undertake to supplement traditional Architects Institute of America (AIA) contracts with provisions applicable to their sustainable projects. Others draft one-off contracts, specific to a given building. Both of those approaches have their merits, but neither is particularly eloquent or efficient. Some groups are working on the development of green-building-specific contracts to replace or supplement the commonly utilized AIA contracts for construction projects. One such example is the ConsensusDOCS 310 Green Building Addendum, prepared by ConsensusDOCS, the AIA's primary competitor in the world of building contracts. The documents contemplate the use of a "Green Building Facilitator" (GBF), whose role it is to effectively serve as the sustainability construction manager. The contracts call for architects and designers to include green building designs and specifications and attempt to discuss liability arising out of green projects. As time passes and it becomes obvious that green building is not merely a fad, other similar sustainable-development-specific contracts are likely to follow.

Assuming that the contract is specific enough and that the owner is able to prove that a contractor or subcontractor breached the contract, another unique question arises in the form of determining the owners' damages. In a traditional construction project, if a glazier uses the wrong windows, the owner can obtain estimates as to the cost of replacing the incorrect windows with the proper model and can easily prove its damages. Or, on the other hand, if the windows are installed improperly and leak, the owner can prove the cost of remedying the issue, plus any damage to property caused by the leaking. But in the case of errors related to construction material, correcting the error might generate *more waste* and be *less sustainable* than simply permitting the error to remain in place. As discussed in chapter 3, if a contractor uses traditional concrete instead of specially formulated concrete that serves to reduce the "heat island" effect of buildings, does the owner really want to tear out all of the concrete and start over?

Many errors or construction-related disputes arise not out of improper materials, but out of a failure to meet expectations. For example, a project might be poorly managed or constructed and might thus fail to meet LEED certification requirements. Or despite the best efforts of all involved, the building might just not be as efficient as it had been predicted to be, and might have higher energy costs than had been forecast.

If the damages are the loss of a clearly defined tax credit applicable to buildings with a certain level of LEED certification, damages would be easy to prove. But if the damages arise out of the use of an improper material or out of somewhat amorphous energy use forecasts, even if the owner can clearly identify the wrongdoer, the owner might face a significant challenge in proving what the wrongdoer's error will ultimately cost. Since at least some of the value of green building is purely subjective, it is unlikely that an owner will ever feel fully compensated for a construction dispute. In the end, the owner will have to rely on the informed estimates of its consultants and try to prove that those estimates are reasonable and not merely a green building penalty.

For attorneys reading these sentences, the concepts should sound vaguely familiar: damages are speculative or difficult to calculate; damages can be reasonably estimated; and estimates are not intended to be a penalty. Those are the cornerstones of liquidated damages. Because of the difficulties in proving actual damages for construction errors, and because the building process already involves a substantial element of contract preparation and vetting, owners should consider inserting liquidated damages clauses into their contracts, at least for certain types of claims. For example, if an incorrect material is used, the owner might specify liquidated damages of three times the difference in price between the improper material used and the material specified by the contract. That is a substantial incentive for contractors to ensure they follow material specifications.

Unfortunately, not all aspects of the building process are so easily reduced to calculation. Even more interesting, many parties that specialize in green building projects now approach the projects with language of their own. For example, in many building projects where the owner *intends* to build a facility with a specified LEED rating, the architect and LEED commissioning agent have demanded to insert clauses in their contracts specifying that they will use reasonable efforts to achieve a certain rating, but that they make no guarantee of any particular outcome. They frequently want owners to relinquish any claim arising out of the building's failure to perform in an energy-efficient fashion or to achieve a desired level of LEED certification. That causes many owners to question exactly why they are paying extra for a green building, if they are not guaranteed to get a certain outcome. Ultimately, the nature of LEED evaluation does not lend itself particularly well to guaranteed outcomes as there are too many variables that even the best-intentioned professionals are unable to control. And unfortunately, the USGBC does not give out awards for effort.

The savvy owner will want to use every effort possible to identify the parties responsible for LEED certification and building performance, and use the contracts at issue to obligate those parties to the greatest extent possible. The savvy owner must also be aware of any state-specific restrictions applicable to green building contracts. For example, Rhode Island recently considered legislation including a provision that "No person, corporation or entity shall be held liable for the failure of a major project to meet the LEED certified standard or other standards established for the project as long as a good faith attempt was made to achieve the standard set for the project."[17] Obviously, that sort of a locality-specific law could dramatically change an owner's (or a contractor's) approach to green building.

The extent to which green building technology can be incorporated into a construction project (or potentially required or encouraged as a component of local or municipal regulations) is practically limitless. Every utility service that is utilized by a building, from electric to natural gas to light and thermal heat, is potentially the subject of a sustainable aspect of a project. When considering either regulations to require/permit the use of sustainable building technology or considering the use of such technology within a building project, one would be well advised to thoroughly research the technology and its benefits and drawbacks.

For example, one of the continually expanding forms of green building technology is the use of "green roofs," either on new projects or as retrofits to existing structures.

> A green roof is commonly defined as a roof that consists of vegetation and soil, or a growing medium, planted over a waterproofing membrane. There are two basic types of green roofs, an extensive roof, which has a few inches of soil cover, and an intensive roof that has two feet or more of soil for a variety of grass, trees, bushes and

---

17. R.I. SB 2009S 0232B, § 37-24-6.

shrubs. Green roofs are used in a multitude of buildings, including industrial facilities, commercial offices, retail property and residences. The benefits of a green roof include reduced storm-water runoff, absorption of air pollution, reduced heat island effect, protection of underlying roof materials from sunlight, reduced noise, and insulation from extreme temperatures. A green roof can thus be a critical design element for a green building.[18]

Green roof projects have found almost universal praise from public and private sources.

> Green roofs use rooftop vegetation and underlying soil to intercept storm water, delay runoff peaks, and reduce runoff discharge rates and volume. . . . Green roofs are becoming an important tool in areas with dense development where the use of other space-intensive storm water management practices, such as detention ponds and large infiltration systems, is impractical.[19]

However, not all green building technologies have met with such success. For example, one emerging building technology is the use of "shower towers" to minimize or replace the use of traditional air conditioning for cooling office buildings. Shower towers are, in effect, airshafts that use recirculating chilled water to reduce air temperature and reduce the demand on HVAC systems.

However, when the city of Melbourne, Australia, built their new, state-of-the-art offices in the "CH2" building and included shower towers, the towers had to be decommissioned and redesigned shortly after construction due to the presence of Legionella within the cooling system. That same building experienced complaints regarding

---

18. Geoffrey White, *Green Roofs & LEED Credits—A Liability Issue?*, Clean Techies Blog (June 24, 2009), http://blog.cleantechies.com/2009/06/24/green-roofs-leed-credits-liability-issue/ (last visited Mar. 1, 2010).
19. U.S. Envtl. Protection Agency, Report to Congress on the Impacts and Control of CSOs and SSOs, ch 8, at 8-18.

noise levels due to "open plan" offices, and complaints regarding a stench from the waterless urinals.[20]

In other words, not all green technology has been universally successful. Accordingly, those contemplating green building technology—again either as a component of a building project or as a potential component for local regulation—must conduct some significant research into the viability of different forms of green building technology and some substantial cost-benefit analysis.

Cost-benefit analysis includes both short-term and long-term analysis. Some of the results from studies of the economics of sustainable building construction techniques have had surprising results. "According to a study by McGraw-Hill Construction, a building's value increases by almost 8%, return on investment improves approximately 7% and occupancy ratio and rent ratio increases grow by more than 3% when 'green' is part of the equation."[21] However, while that study did generally review "return on investment," it did not engage in substantial analysis as to whether the increased return was based on actual, objective building performance (e.g., energy savings) or was based on subjective factors—such as tenant desirability to live or work in a "green" building.

Those who have looked at objective building performance have had mixed results. For example, Dartmouth College went to significant expense several years ago in order to improve and certify five buildings under the LEED standard—only to find that the buildings did not perform according to energy-modeling predictions. Dartmouth representatives have reported that the buildings are performing better than other, non-LEED buildings, but they are not meeting the energy

---

20. Clay Lucas & Cameron Houston, *Civic Showpiece Failing to Deliver*, Aug. 27, 2007, http://www.theage.com.au/news/national/civic-showpiece-failing-to-deliver/2007/08/28/1188067111145.html (last visited Feb. 28, 2010).

21. Press Release, Energy Ace, Energy Ace Inc. to Offer the Industry's First Guarantee for LEED (Aug. 12, 2009) http://www.elephantjournal.com/2009/08/why-leed/ (last visited Mar. 5, 2010).

modeling or energy parameters that design teams contemplated during the design stage.[22]

Similarly, the recently constructed Youngstown, Ohio, Federal Building was intended to be a green building and features extensive use of natural light, a reflective white roof, and other similar features that were used to obtain LEED certification upon construction. However, in actual use, the building has failed to obtain Energy Star status with the US EPA. "The building's cooling system, a major gas guzzler, was one culprit. Another was its design: to get its LEED label, it racked up points for things like native landscaping rather than structural energy-saving features, according to a study by the General Services Administration, which owns the building."[23]

In one LEED building, the owners undertook a postconstruction investigation into why the building was not producing the electrical efficiency gains promised by the LEED consultants working on the project. They discovered that the "design stage" electricity consumption calculations were based solely on electrical use by lights and HVAC systems. In other words, the designers had not accounted for electricity use by the computers, servers, refrigerators, and other appliances that were to be used by building occupants. The building, standing empty by itself, may have had impressive electrical efficiency. But the cost of operation, as measured by the owner, failed to produce any improvement over a formerly occupied, traditionally constructed building, because the design calculations on operating costs ignored the largest electrical loads that the building would have: its occupants.

The USGBC has not taken these real-world results lying down. Rather, it has worked to develop a Building Performance Initiative,

---

22. Tatiana Cooke, *LEED-Certified Projects Fall Short of Projections*, The Dartmouth (Sept. 25, 2009), http://thedartmouth.com/2009/09/25/news/leed/ (last visited Feb. 28, 2010).

23. Mireya Navarro, *Some Buildings Not Living Up to Green Label*, Aug. 30, 2009, http://www.nytimes.com/2009/08/31/science/earth/31leed.html?pagewanted=all (last visited Oct. 13, 2011).

aimed at the development of comprehensive building performance data collection from all buildings that have achieved LEED certification, which data would be analyzed and used to provide feedback to building owners and which would be used to update LEED specifications based on real-world results.[24]

Building occupants have not taken the issue of nonperforming green buildings lightly, either. For example, the owners of newly constructed, LEED certified buildings have filed claims against architects and LEED consultants when buildings have failed to perform. In one instance, a LEED building was advertised as having superior air quality based upon advanced air handling equipment and superior insulation; a tenant in that building filed a claim alleging that the superior insulation actually resulted in more employee sick days.[25] In another case, a building owner marketed the project, preconstruction, as a building that was to be LEED Gold-certified (in an effort to obtain higher rents and higher occupancy rates).[26] However, when budget and time constraints prevented the project from achieving the desired level of certification, the owner brought claims against the architect

---

24. Press Release, USGBC, USGBC Tackles Building Performance Head On (Aug. 26, 2009), http://www.prweb.com/releases/usgbc/building_performance/prweb2791024.htm (last visited Feb. 28, 2010).

25. Henry E. Powderly II, *Green Industry Tills Fertile Ground for Lawsuits*, Sept. 5, 2008, http://libn.com/blog/2008/09/05/green-industry-tills-fertile-ground-for-lawsuits/ (last visited Mar. 10, 2010).

26. While they are beyond the scope of this article, tenants considering finding space in a sustainable building should consider use of a green building lease. In brief, "A green lease is needed from the owner's perspective to ensure that their investment is protected and from the tenant's perspective to ensure that the owner constructs and operates the building in a manner that ensures energy efficiency." Rich Cartlidge, *Use a Green Lease Less You Lose Out*, Dec. 29, 2009, http://www.greenbuildingpro.com/news/51-green-news-archives/1032-use-a-green-lease-less-you-lose-out (last visited Oct. 13, 2011). Green building leases are described at length in the book, *Green Building and Sustainable Development*, offered by the American Bar Association, edited by Jonathan E. Furr, Nicole C. Kibert, James T. Mayer, and Shannon D. Sentman.

and LEED consultants based on projected rent reductions and occupancy losses.[27]

Insurance companies have started offering green-building-specific builder's risk insurance. In recognition of the fact that green building construction involves a substantial amount of subjective value in the form of public relations, AIG now offers insurance coverage insuring green buildings against "adverse publicity" associated with performance issues.[28] For every potential new risk, insurance companies are finding opportunities to earn premiums—often insuring against risks that are difficult, if not impossible, to objectively define with any real certainty.

One final risk that must be considered with respect to green building projects is the long-term risk associated with the use of any building: future damage and potential renovations. In undertaking a building project, nearly every owner is familiar with the concept that risk of loss for the building will be, at some point, squarely with the building owner. That is a risk that nearly every building owner insures against, and most insurance policies contemplate indemnifying the owner from repair/replacement costs for the building, up to the face value of the insurance policy.

With respect to a green building project, the owner must carefully consider this insurance need. Often, a sustainable building project has greater construction costs associated with it, compared to a "traditional" or "less sustainable" process. That might mean the costs of building repair or replacement would be inflated compared to the traditional buildings that insurers are accustomed to.

Accordingly, building owners must make sure that the insurance policies obtained for a green building provide enough coverage to

<hr>

27. Furr et al., *supra* note 26.
28. *Lawyer: First LEED-Related Lawsuit in U.S. Tip of Iceberg*, Jan. 15, 2009, http://www.environmentalleader.com/2009/01/15/lawyer-first-leed-related-lawsuit-in-us-tip-of-iceberg (last visited Mar. 1, 2010).

fund repairs performed in the same sustainable fashion as the building's original construction was performed. In addition, the building owner must ensure that the insurance policies _require_ any insured repairs to be completed in a sustainable fashion. Customarily, a policy may require repairs to be completed according to custom and practice in the industry, or in a workmanlike fashion. Unless sustainable building practices become the rule instead of the exception, this language would not protect the owner of a green building and would not guarantee that insured repairs are completed in a green manner commensurate with the remainder of the building.

The field of green building is relatively new, spanning little over a decade compared to centuries of development of traditional insurance and construction models. Much of what is discussed today in terms of how green buildings will be built, regulated, and occupied is anecdotal. It is the next 20 years that will show whether green building is a fashionable trend or is truly—pardon the pun—sustainable.

However, in considering any aspect of sustainable construction projects, the single most important thing to keep in mind is how the sustainable aspects of the project bleed into every other aspect of the project. In many ways, those with minimal experience on traditional construction projects make the best owners of "green" buildings as they approach the project with no preconceived notions about how the process should work (or how it should be insured, utilized, etc.). These building novices are open to new ideas and frequently are better at conceptualizing how the green/sustainable aspect of the project needs to impact every other component thereof.

IT ALL COMES TOGETHER

Regardless of the nature of the project that a community or a private developer undertakes, and frankly, regardless of whether the project is intended to be sustainable or not, there are a number of simple, concrete steps that can be taken in the earliest stage of project planning. These simple steps will play a significant role in determining whether the project will be a success or not.

First, whoever is responsible for planning the project must clearly define what their goal for the project is. Is the project to have more than one purpose, or is it going to be integrated and interoperable with a larger system? Is the project intended to serve any social or environmental goals in addition to the practical underlying purpose for the project?

If sustainability is a consideration, is the goal to erect a building that achieves a certain degree of LEED certification (for example, to obtain a specified tax benefit provided to LEED-certified buildings), or something else? Is the goal to reduce construction costs, operating costs, or a combination thereof? Is the sustainability goal best viewed as a short-term goal to produce a quick, easy, tangible green project to publicize, or is it part of a comprehensive, longer-term approach to sustainable policies?

What does the community define as sustainable? Is it a holistic approach to the project or an effort to address some limited, specific deficiency (e.g., an effort to reduce use of potable water)? It is nothing short of shocking how many large-scale projects begin without a clear definition of the goals and objectives. Frequently, communities undertake a project and understand that the goal is to "build a police station" or "develop a subdivision," without viewing that limited goal in a larger context and without having criteria in place to help evaluate decisions that arise through the project's path to completion.

Once those goals are identified, the next step is to start assembling the core team of people who will be responsible for planning the project, making decisions as the project goes forward, and making the initial evaluations about whether and how the project is satisfying its goals. This core team must be clearly informed of what the goals are and must be given the ability to develop an approach to the job that will enable the project to succeed. In many instances, this means that a project owner has to bring more professionals into the project at an earlier stage than she might otherwise do—but it is essential for each member of the team (engineer, architect, attorney, etc.) to have a frank discussion about the project and the goals *before the project has begun in any meaningful way.* From a legal perspective, understanding the risks and obstacles that the engineer or architect perceives with respect to the project is invaluable and will guide the attorney's efforts to draft project-related documentation and contracts.

Once initial goals are defined and the initial team is established, with respect to sustainable developments, one of the best practices to implement is to have a discussion not only about the project's composition and goals, but also how to incentivize the project. Incentives can come in all forms: incentives for contractors to perform work in a sustainable fashion; financing incentives to encourage private development; available loans or grants to reduce the cost of the project; incentives to encourage others to follow in the sustainable path set by the project and make it a working example for others—the possibilities are endless. This thinking should be—pardon the cliché—outside of the box. If the project team can identify a potential problem, they can identify an incentive and solution to avoid that problem. If the concern is use of improper materials, the contract can provide powerful incentives for contractors to use the appropriate material. If the concern is long-term maintenance of sustainable aspects of the project, ordinances, bonds, or back-up/dormant financing sources can be built into the project to ensure its long-term success.

The mind-set described above is not limited just to sustainable projects. The sustainable technologies described in this book came about when parties working on a project collaborated to find a better, more efficient, more expansive solution to an existing problem. This mind-set of collaboration and creativity, and the willingness to embrace new ideas can form the foundation of any successful project. But if sustainable development, whether public or private, is to have any meaningful effect for our communities and for the communities of tomorrow, it must be more than a hollow gesture. The laws of nature are fixed and immutable; communities have a finite set of resources at their disposal. By using those resources more wisely, communities can be stronger, more efficient, and more likely to have an impact not only on today, but on the long road to tomorrow.

Index